BECAUSE ADULTHOOD SHOULDN'T BE THIS BORING

A Rebellion Against the Fun Police

SHANELLE FRANKLIN

Shanelle Franklin
First Edition 2026

Copyright © 2025 Shanelle Franklin

The right of Shanelle Franklin to be identified as the author of the work has been asserted by her in accordance with the Copyright, Designs and Patents Act 1988.

All rights reserved. This book is sold subject to the condition that no part of this book is to be reproduced, in any shape or form, or by way of trade, stored in a retrieval system or transmitted in any form or by any means, electronic, mechanical, photocopying, recording, be lent, re-sold, hired out or otherwise circulated in any form of binding or cover other than that in which it is published and without a similar condition, including this condition, being imposed on the subsequent purchaser, without prior permission of the copyright holder.

Typeset by 2QT Publishing Services
Cover design by Charlotte Mouncey
Cover images from iStockphoto.com attributed to Togapix ©

Publisher Disclaimer:
The Publisher does not hold any responsibility for any inaccuracies or opinions expressed by the author. Any enquiries should be directed to the author.

Printed by IngramSparks (Australia)

ISBN: 978-1-7643776-0-7

To Summer & Ollie – my loves!
You showed me what I could never quite see on my own 🤟

CONTENTS

INTRODUCTION	7
CHAPTER ONE - A QUICK DETOUR	13
CHAPTER TWO - WHAT HAVE WE BEEN MISSING?	18
CHAPTER THREE - OUR MAGNIFICENT BRAINS	38
CHAPTER FOUR - HAHA!	50
CHAPTER FIVE - WHAT'S IN YOUR CAULDRON?	59
CHAPTER SIX - CLOCK YOURSELF	76
CHAPTER SEVEN - CURIOSITY DID NOT KILL THE CAT	83
CHAPTER EIGHT - WHAT STANDS IN OUR WAY?	91
CHAPTER NINE - BACK SEAT DRIVER	104
CHAPTER TEN - FRIENDSHIP	114
CHAPTER ELEVEN - EMOTIONS ARE THEIR OWN WILD BEASTS	124
CHAPTER TWELVE - THE SECRECT WEAPON	140
CHAPTER THIRTEEN - YOUR SUPERPOWER	148
CHAPTER FOURTEEN - FREE YOURSELF FROM THE CHAINS THAT BIND ~ Chaka Khan	159
FINAL WORDS	166
ACKNOWLEDGEMENTS	173
REFERENCES	175

INTRODUCTION

Do the best you can until you know better. Then when you know better, do better.
~ Maya Angelou ~

Words are my love language.

On the surface, they may seem simple – just ink on a page or sounds in the air – but their power lies in how they make us and others feel. Words don't just speak meaning; they shape it.

Have you ever read something that stopped you cold? A line that hit so deep it felt like it was written just for you. Or a sentence so close to home it echoed your own unspoken thoughts? In that moment, it's as if the writer reached inside you, pulled out something raw and real, and you had no choice but to sit with it.

That's why I love words. When something that feels like 'truth' is spoken and it strikes a chord, it's because that wisdom already lives somewhere inside you. It's a feeling that grabs you by the shoulders and holds you still – not to paralyse, but to tune you into it.

While I'm not a scientist by training, this book is firmly grounded in scientific evidence. My background is in communication, and what I lack in lab credentials I make up for with relentless curiosity and a knack for spotting patterns in human behaviour. I follow the breadcrumbs of questions until something clicks – and what I uncovered has been both illuminating and, in many ways, a total game changer.

One of my strongest (and sometimes most exhausting) skills is that I can read a room to within an inch of its life. Micro-expressions, energy shifts, awkward silences – I pick them up like Wi-Fi. If someone's vibe is off, even by half a degree, I've already clocked it, filed it, and probably overthought it. I call it my built-in radar system.

I'm not big on labels (unless they come with laundry instructions), but if I had to choose a few, I'd say I'm empathic and an extroverted introvert. I know – sounds like a walking contradiction, right? That's because it totally is.

I'm the kind of person who gets excited to go out, has the best time while I'm there, and then needs a solid three business days to emotionally recharge. I feel things deeply – like, 'my brain is running a full-season reality show' deeply.

It's a gift when it helps me connect with people. And sure, sometimes it's a bit of a burden – like when I randomly start replaying a slightly awkward conversation from five years ago while trying to fall asleep.

Here's the upside: curiosity, empathy, and emotional attunement don't just make you sensitive – they make you a decoder of human nuance. You start to see the little tells in people's stories, the moments when someone lights up or shuts down. And that kind of awareness helps build bridges, soften judgements, and remind us that everyone's carrying something – usually just beneath the surface.

I like to think of my brain as a shared apartment with two very different roommates.

One's the life of the party. She thrives on connection, lives for cracking jokes, swapping stories, and riding the high of a group chat that's absolutely on fire. The other? She's the quiet one who slips away to recharge.

Both are real. For a long time I thought I had to pick a side; be either the social butterfly or the empath. But now? I've learned to appreciate the rhythm they create.

One fuels my spark to show up and engage. The other gently taps me on the shoulder like, 'Hey … maybe let's wind it back in.' I've learned that, through years of doing it wrong and not understanding those wonderful things called boundaries.

I was born to talk and connect – that much is crystal clear.

Back in school, I used to cringe every time I got thrown out of class for talking too much. Later, friends or colleagues would lob their polite little jabs about my chit-chat. But here's the thing: I also love listening. So, I get the balance. I've always known that one of my strengths is connecting with people through words, and over time, I turned that strength into a career I'm genuinely proud of.

I've worked hard to get to this point – and I fully embrace it. Because under all that talking was always one simple desire: to be understood.

This isn't some 'I've got it all figured out' speech. I don't have all the answers, and some of the things that have worked wonders for me might not work for you.

My husband Dan calls himself a positive realist – and, well, it sounded good, so I copied him. The things I've discovered came from tuning into the sparks of curiosity that had been quietly lurking in the background. I kept following where the research took me and believed that if a book, docuseries, or podcast landed in front of me, maybe the universe was feeding me exactly what I was craving.

I was craving answers – to why so many people around me were unhappy, getting sick, or running out of steam. We're not living the way we truly want to. We were – and sometimes still are – miserable as sin.

So, I went digging. And I found some answers. I tested them like any good student would – and they worked. I even roped in friends for a few of my random experiments, and the results spoke for themselves. More on that later.

In this book – my very first one (no pressure!) – I'm sharing why learning to spark your own happiness on purpose might just be the surprising little pick-me-up you didn't see coming. And it starts with your own curiosity.

You may be thinking, 'Yeah, yeah, I know what curiosity is.'

But my question is: are you really listening to it?

When we let curiosity take the wheel, it steers us to unexpected, joyful places – the kind that spark pure, no-strings-attached fun.

Why playful fun, you may ask? Because it's the real kind of happy, not the 'I just scrolled through Instagram for two hours like a raccoon on an iPhone and now my soul has left the building' kind of happy. I'm talking about proper joy – the type that doesn't need Wi-Fi, doesn't drain your battery, and doesn't leave you feeling like you've just eaten a bag of emotional chips. It's the joy that reminds you you're alive and worth taking care of.

This book won't magically fix all your problems – like that annoying parent at school drop-off or your piss-taking boss (I'm no guru). And it's definitely not here to guilt-trip you into action either.

What it is here for is to offer ideas on how to trigger your happiness, on purpose, with purpose. How? With tools. Real, usable tools. And just as importantly, a solid excuse to use them. You'll find those here – plus, hopefully, a few laughs along the way.

Let's face it: not one of us is single-handedly fixing the world – unless, of course, you've got a cape and a secret identity no one knows about. What we can do is start right where we are – in our own backyard. Not literally (unless you love gardening), but by figuring out what makes you feel like you're actually living your life.

And if you're not sure what that is? No worries – we'll hunt it down together.

Here's the cool part: every time someone starts showing up for themselves, it sends out this quiet little ripple. Before you know it, other people start doing the same. Kind of like emotional peer pressure, but the good kind. This tends to make everyone around you want to be a little happier, too.

You've probably heard the saying 'put your own life vest on first.' It makes sense here – because if the lifeguard's going under, no one's getting saved. So, get yourself steady, take a breath, and then be that person who brings the fun.

In this book, we'll explore how seeking your kind of fun can trigger your happiness. We'll uncover what's holding you back, help you discover your unique path to joy, and find ways to reclaim that time that always seems to be MIA. Expect a blend of science, ancient wisdom, a touch of the woo-woo, and lots of relatable content. As Byron Katie says, 'The work you do on yourself has power as it is applied by each person.' Knowledge alone isn't enough; it's about how you apply it. Test it out. Trust how it makes you feel.

Playful stuff connects you to that spark inside – the bit that still knows how to be happy. And honestly, your brain's always learning, no matter how old you are. Who's to say the things you'll fall in love with aren't still out there, just waiting for you to stumble across them?

For whatever reason, you and I found each other. I hope this book is a little reminder that your happiness matters. Getting to know yourself better isn't always smooth sailing, but you won't look back once you start giving time and care to the person who truly deserves it – you.

By initiating fun through play, I've uncovered the real me – kinder, lighter, and, most importantly, a better friend to myself. Former forest monk Björn Natthiko Lindeblad spoke beautifully about the importance of becoming a better friend to yourself, because you are your longest and most loyal companion.

To share a friendship like that with yourself is like offering your own heart a warm hug. Yet the sad truth is that this is often the most neglected relationship of all. We forget that we're not just living with ourselves; we're also living as ourselves. Learning to have fun, to laugh more, and to enjoy the little things is how we start to remember the joy of our own company.

We often talk about a loneliness epidemic in the world, but what's rarely mentioned is the loneliness we feel within - the quiet disconnection from ourselves. Joyful fun is truly an antidote, not just to that but to so many other things we'll explore together. Cliché, I know ... but it really is the gift that keeps on giving.

I'm riding a feeling here – and something tells me we're in sync, searching for the same thing: connection, joy, maybe even a little magic. So ... let's dive down the rabbit hole together.

CHAPTER ONE

A QUICK DETOUR

As you start to walk on the way, the way appears.
- Rumi -

How did I end up here, writing this book? Well, it all started with a curious mind and a burning question: why was I spending most of my time in the 'red' zone – overworked, overstimulated, and on the verge of burnout? Not ideal for an empath.

The 'green' zone, on the other hand – that calm, content, in-control space – felt like a distant dream. My boundaries and priorities? A total mess.

But the more I paid attention, the more I realised I wasn't alone. The world these days feels like one giant group chat you can't leave. It's loud, chaotic, and everyone's shouting over each other. The constant stream of the world's problems flooding our feeds can feel totally overwhelming - and because we're so plugged in, so endlessly connected, it starts to feel like it's all ours to carry.

LIGHTS, CAMERA ... CHAOS

I've spent years navigating the media landscape as a presenter, producer, and MC – collecting more job titles than LinkedIn knows what to do with. Storytelling is my craft, and making people laugh is my favourite thing to do. At heart, I'm a creative soul, always chasing real connection.

I've thrown myself into the opportunistic ring more times than I can count, taken hits that rattled my confidence, and knockdowns that stung. But every closed door was just another round bell – time to reset and step through the next opening to see where it would take me.

I've learned to embrace these twists and turns, because somehow the universe always seemed to know what it was doing. Trusting the process wasn't easy – especially when you can't see the wood for the trees and just feel plain vulnerable.

School was an interesting time. If given the choice to go back to those days instead of being an adult, I'd decline without hesitation. I felt restless. I hadn't found my spark and was running on autopilot – knowing there was something more for me but feeling stuck in the system.

I'm also mildly annoyed at myself for not being drawn to a career that felt, you know … easier to attain. Something with a clear path, a retirement plan, and maybe even a mug with my name on it. But no – I chose media. A thrilling, unstable, emotionally exhausting rollercoaster with all the structure of a sandcastle in a windstorm. Success isn't guaranteed – but imposter syndrome, oh, that shows up right on time.

After school, I pursued a communications degree just to tick a box. But I didn't expect it to actually spark anything. Then radio came along – the perfect mix of my love for music and talking. It lit me up. It felt like I'd found my thing. The problem? You can't just study it and waltz into a job. It's one of those 'right place, right time, hustle forever' kind of gigs. And every time I wanted to throw in the towel, some pesky gut feeling kept pulling me back. It was probably a blend of sheer stubbornness and those perfect 'right place, right time' moments that kept the fire burning.

Honestly, it became an obsession – one that nearly drove me around the bend. I had the patience of a flea and, truth be told, I was my own worst enemy. A sensitive, empathic soul and a classic overthinker, I didn't realise I was standing squarely in my own way.

What I lacked most was something simple: a passion outside of work.

Dan used to nag me about work-life balance, and I'd roll my eyes, thinking, 'What would he know? He's not a creative artist like me.' Turns out, it doesn't matter who you are – everyone needs something that lifts them out of the ordinary, that lets them step beyond their day-to-day roles and limitations. And when you find that missing piece in your own puzzle, trust me, you'll wonder how you ever lived without it. So … thanks, Dannyboy. Sometimes the people closest to us see what's right in front of us while we're too busy being distracted to notice.

FUN? NEVER HEARD OF HER

I used to think balance meant clocking out of work and straight into mum mode with my kids, Summer and Ollie. But life doesn't hand you a neat little schedule – it throws an entire wardrobe of hats at you: parent, partner, friend, co-worker, cleaner, snack provider, emotional support human – doer of all the things. In the chaos of juggling them all, I missed the most important ingredient: finding fun.

You know, the thing that lets you 'let some air out of your tyres,' 'take a load off,' or just chill the F out. Turns out, playful fun isn't just for kids – it's essential. It reduces stress, boosts creativity, and tops up the energy tank we keep trying to run on empty.

What did I notice? How good I felt after it.

The key was not to wait to feel better to start having fun – you need fun to feel better. We sometimes have it the wrong way around.

Do the fun thing to snap you out of the funk!

MERCURY, MATCHA, AND MILD MADDNESS

The terms 'wellness' and 'balance' used to get me all hot and bothered. Achieving balance felt like trying to juggle flaming swords while riding a unicycle on a tightrope. And if I so much as glanced at a stressor, the whole equilibrium would collapse like a house of cards in a hurricane. Feeling stressed about achieving balance is completely counterproductive.

For example, the pressure to choose the right milk, and now we've started giving bread the side-eye in the supermarket. (I still love you, bread, but apparently, we aren't allowed to talk.) We also have those judgemental, pushy watches on our wrists that nag us to move if we so much as sit down for coffee with a friend or sneak in a micro-Netflix binge.

It's no surprise that maintaining mental stability in today's fast-paced, stress-fuelled, goal-driven hustle is challenging. To be honest, I grew tired of feeling miserable. And the worst part? I had caused it – or rather, allowed it. But I realised I could also fix it. I began to reflect on when I felt my happiest. It was almost always when I was doing something I enjoyed, something that absorbed me completely. When you finally find that missing piece in your puzzle, trust me, you'll never look back.

Multitasking also isn't the answer. You think you're responding to emails while cooking, but you're really just setting off the smoke alarm while sending your boss a message about 'grilled deadlines.' Next minute, you're doom-scrolling, watching a reel that says Mercury is in retrograde, and that explains EVERYTHING! It's always a solid excuse but letting poor Mercury cop the blame won't solve the issue most of us are facing.

We're driving ourselves mad trying to cut corners, swap out ingredients, and spend a small fortune on everything social media tells us we need – just in case we somehow turn into a crappier version of ourselves without it. 'How can this be?' we cry. 'I drink matcha tea, shovel wheatgrass into my mouth by the bucketload, and haven't touched bread since 2022!' All while still convincing ourselves we only drink one to two units of alcohol per week. (Props to you if you actually do this … or if you're teetotal.) And zero judgement if you don't – I had a rude awakening when I discovered that units don't mean glasses!

Many of us are restless, caught in a cycle of fluctuating between satisfaction and dissatisfaction. We often imagine scenarios like, 'Once this happens, I'll feel good' – a delusion of grandeur, such as sailing around the Adriatic coast with your two best pals. However, the reality rarely matches the mental image we've created. For instance, the boat trip you booked gets rained out, and the seagulls seem to have a vendetta against your vessel and your cheese platter. We forget that happy experiences can't just live in our heads; we need to create the physical experience, rather than dreaming them up to a level of unrealistic perfection.

Here's a fun fact: did you know there's only one way to experience happiness? Bold claim, I know, but it's one that historian Yuval Noah Harari has studied extensively. Here's the science: when we engage in activities we enjoy, our happy hormones steamroll through our bloodstream, setting off a firework display of electric signals in our brain. Sounds like a party, right? Because it is. This biochemical reaction is what triggers the feeling of happiness.

Having a laugh and just playing around sounds simple, right? But for some reason, we hesitate to find ways to make it happen. What stories are we telling ourselves that stop us from making fun a priority? The truth is that adults need play just as much as kids do. Yet things like busy schedules and endless to-do lists often push it right to the bottom.

So maybe the real question is: what are we skipping over without even noticing?

CHAPTER TWO
WHAT HAVE WE BEEN MISSING?

We don't stop playing because we grow old; we grow old because we stop playing.
~ George Bernard Shaw ~

Quick side note: your mind might create some resistance to this because the solution is quite simple. Don't pull away or challenge it just because it seems too good to be true. Stay with me, and I'll prove it – or at least the science will.

People often mix up joy and happiness, but they're not quite the same. Happiness is usually that little buzz you get when something good happens – like nailing a goal, being recognised for your work, or grabbing a custard tart on the way home (highly recommend). The thing is it doesn't always stick around. It comes and goes depending on what's happening around you.

Joy, though – that's different. Joy feels quieter, deeper. It's the steady feeling you get when you're watching your kids sleep, creating something that lights you up, or just sitting outside with the sun on your face. It can be there even when life isn't smooth sailing.

Brené Brown puts it perfectly: 'Joy is more vulnerable than happiness – many of us are afraid to feel it fully because we fear it won't last.' And she's right. Happiness is like a quick spark, but joy… joy feels like home.

FEELINGS: THE UNWANTED GUESTS WHO NEVER LEAVE

Mental health isn't a puzzle you need to solve; it's just part of being human. Some days feel lighter, some heavier, and that's completely normal. Like our bodies, our minds shift with our experiences, relationships, and the world around us. I'm not talking about medically diagnosed mental disorders here, but the everyday, circumstantial stuff – the times when we don't even realise we're standing in our own way.

Some days we feel steady and strong. Other days, we're anxious, overwhelmed, or stuck in darker headspaces. That doesn't mean we're broken – it just means we're human. Honestly, some days keeping your socks matching is a win.

Looking after our mental health isn't about finding a finish line – it's ongoing. It's noticing when we're slipping into unhelpful patterns, understanding what triggers us, and slowly building tools that help us reset. For some, that's movement. For others, it's rest, creativity, connection – or just having fun for the sake of it (because fun really is therapeutic).

There's no one-size-fits-all formula. The goal isn't to be 'cured,' but to live well with our minds and meet ourselves with compassion along the way, something we often neglect. Maybe it's because it's a soft word, one we tend to cast aside.

Holy heck, though, I love that word – compassion. It's such a tonic. The more you use it on yourself, the stronger it becomes.

THE ART OF NOT LOSING YOUR SHIT

When we, as adults, hear the words 'play' or 'light-hearted fun,' it often feels like something left behind with juice boxes and Velcro shoes – a relic of childhood, like nap time or believing quicksand would be a bigger problem in life. We think we know what play is: games like hide and seek, pillow fights, or the high-stakes survival sport of 'the floor is lava' – where one wrong step meant certain doom (or at least, you're in trouble for using mum's fancy linen cushion as a makeshift lily pad).

Let's take a leaf from the animal kingdom: adult animals place a high importance on play because, frankly, life in the wild is exhausting – dodging predators, finding food, and pretending to be interested in the same three squirrels every day. Sometimes you just need to chase your tail, splash in a puddle, or fake-wrestle your bestie to keep it together. For animals, play is like yoga, therapy, and a group chat roast session all rolled into one. It keeps them sharp, social, and slightly less grumpy. Plus, if you've ever seen an adult elephant bodysurfing in mud or a dolphin playing fetch with seaweed, it's pretty clear: even in the animal kingdom, grown-ups need recess too.

Nature will always serve up good medicine if only we pause to notice.

A dear friend of mine, Sharmaine – a proud Murri woman who lovingly calls me her sister – taught me that Aboriginal Elders play regularly because play isn't just for the young, it's a powerful way to teach, connect, and keep culture alive. Through playful storytelling, games, dancing, and even a cheeky joke or two, Elders pass down wisdom in ways that are engaging and memorable – think dreamtime stories. Play helps build trust with younger generations, creating a space where learning feels natural and joyful. It's also a reminder that laughter and connection are sacred parts of community life. Elders know that keeping a playful spirit isn't about acting young – it's about staying connected to tradition, to each other, and to the joy that's always been at the heart of culture.

So, what is play? Play is one of the best ways to trigger a state of happiness; it's no-strings-attached fun, which looks and feels joyous. Put simply, it's where your spirit can run free (thank you, Rick Rubin). Play isn't goal-oriented and doesn't require an outcome. There's no right or wrong way to do it, no tests, no rules, and no boundaries. It even grants us the rare gift of freedom from judgement.

We are born with an instinct for curiosity and play; we don't grow out of it. However, we block these impulses as we grow older. But why do we do that?

We know how incredibly beneficial play is for young children, yet we often abandon it, dismissing it as unproductive or frivolous. There's always something more pressing, like what I call our 'doom lists.' Much like doomscrolling, these lists are endless. And it's not just the lists – what about caring for elderly parents, building a career, or raising young children?

Recently, my sister and I were chatting, and we both agreed: by the time our kids become independent, our parents will likely need us more. Do we ever get a break? (More on time in the *Clock Yourself* chapter.)

Something that holds us back as adults is that we struggle to reach our fun states as easily as children do. But the reality is, it's not actually that hard – we just make it hard.

Now, I'm not saying we should all sit on the floor playing with blocks, banging pots and pans or doodling on walls. What I mean is: find something you enjoy doing. Something that feels good for no other reason than it allows you to feel good in the present moment.

Researchers have proven that felt emotions such as joy and excitement reduce inflammation and increase the parts of our brain that control intelligence and stabilise our emotions. Sounds solid, doesn't it? I want to fill you in as to why the stakes are so high. You may be thinking this fun stuff is all well and good, but why is it so important?

The world – and its human inhabitants – have reached an existential crisis. All is not well. Jonathan Haidt describes this perfectly in his book *The Anxious Generation*: 'People don't get depressed when they face threats collectively; they get depressed when they feel isolated, lonely, or useless.'

Dr. Gabor Maté – physician, trauma and addiction expert, and respected author – says:

'In the most health-obsessed society ever, all is not well. At the pinnacle of medical ingenuity, we are seeing more chronic illness, physical afflictions, mental illness, and addictions.'

Forget misspent youth – what about misspent adult years? Roughly two-thirds of the world's eight billion people are expected to die prematurely. Why is that? What are we missing? We continue to face alarming mental health statistics, estimating that one in three women and one in five men will experience major depression in their lifetime. Loneliness is now considered an epidemic. A huge portion of the global population is unwell, not just physically, but emotionally and mentally.

Depression and anxiety are fast becoming two of the biggest challenges of the twenty-first century. So how is it that, on one side of the coin, we're 'healthier' than ever regarding medical advancements … and on the other, drowning in our own minds? Green juice diets vs. unprecedented sadness. Something doesn't add up.

Heart disease is the leading cause of death worldwide. Often, our immune systems become weakened because we live in a chronic, unnatural state of stress. Over time, this stress can trigger disease. The good news? Our bodies have an incredible ability to heal and regenerate – if we give them the chance. According to Dr. Joe Dispenza, stress is a major contributor to heart disease, but engaging in playful fun can help regulate the rhythmic beating of our hearts. How magical is that!

If you're fuelling your body with good sleep and nutrition but still feel a little off – yep, you're not imagining it. Consider how much joy and light-hearted play you might be missing. Honestly, it's just as important as all the other stuff people won't stop making a fuss about – like kale and intermittent fasting.

TRIGGER

I'm keen to discuss the word *trigger*. It's a heavy word, often carrying negative connotations – and rightfully so. We need it to help us understand that jolt when reminded of our Big T and Little T (traumas), and I don't want to discredit its powerful role in acknowledging pain. But consider this: what if we learned to trigger our own happiness through the power of fun? After all, there are always two sides to every story.

If you haven't yet discovered what you can lean into to spark that feeling of happiness, this is the moment to take a step back and let curiosity guide you there. Once we've gathered the right tools - the things that bring us genuine joy – we can call on them to lift our mood. We'll tackle the steps once we've unpacked the full scope of the problem.

When we are triggered by stress, this is what happens: think of it like your body flipping a switch from 'calm' to 'holy shit.' But the good news is that figuring out what triggers a state of happiness for you can help you hit the snooze button on your amygdala (the brain's alarm system) and tell it to take a load off.

When you engage in true fun through the art of play, it becomes a secret weapon to combat stress. One thing that blew my mind was when Dr. Mindy Pelz, author and fasting expert, asked: 'Are you concerned about your belly fat?' If the answer is yes, her next question was: 'What are your stress levels like?'

She further added that we live in one of the most toxic times in human history. Women are applying over 200 toxic, carcinogenic chemicals to their skin every day. The body doesn't know what to do with this overload, so it stores it around the belly and chest. Now, this has nothing to do with play, but I was as shocked as you might be.

When we talk about stress and how to flip ourselves out of that state, playful fun is a proven antidote.

As modern-day parents, we can be hypocritical. I mean, we tell our kids to 'go outside and play' while we sit on the couch, doomscrolling and sipping our third coffee like it's a personality trait. Guilty as charged over here. That's what sent me spiralling down the rabbit hole of 'seeking fun' and its surprisingly medicinal benefits. Spoiler alert: it's not just for kids, and it's cheaper than therapy.

I would yell down the hallway, 'C'mon, screen time's over, go outside and play!' I'm usually met with an eye roll and a grunt, but Summer and Ollie eventually follow suit. They protest about being bored for a while … until an idea hits, and off they go. Watching them dive into a playful game together is just beautiful, until they catch me smiling at them for no apparent reason. That's when I hear them mutter under their breath, 'Mum's being weird, don't look at her.'

But here's the thing: kids learn by what they see. As much as we watch our children to see what they do with their lives, they're also watching us to see what we do with ours. Honestly, I'm still watching my parents to see what they do with theirs.

As Joyce Maynard said, 'I can't tell my children to reach for the sun. All I can do is reach for it myself.' In other words, the best way to show your children the importance of play and joy is to actively engage in it yourself. When you prioritise fun and fulfilment, they learn by example.

If we constantly neglect our own needs, what message are we really sending? That joy is optional? That adulthood means sacrificing happiness? That's not the lesson we want to pass on.

And here's an important reminder: you don't have to spend all your playtime with your kids to model this behaviour. Whether it's enjoying time with friends, diving into a solo hobby, or laughing over a game with your partner, what matters is that they see you embracing joy in all its forms. That variety is essential – it not only helps you build stronger connections with the people you love but also teaches your children what a full, balanced life looks like.

I once heard British presenter Fearne Cotton say that because she works a lot, when she's home, she just plonks herself down and joins whatever play her daughter is engaged in. I thought, that's what I need to do: just sit my bum down and ask if I can be part of what's happening. That advice made a huge difference for me with Summer and Ollie, especially since I really feel the pinch when I travel for work. I love my job – don't get me wrong – but the downside (because there's always one) is that I miss moments with my kids.

My mum still tells me, 'One of the greatest gifts you can give your children is your time.' When you do something fun together, and they get to see you being vulnerable, silly, funny, even a little competitive, that's how lasting memories are made. And the same applies to moments with your friends, partner, parents, or even co-workers. Those shared experiences, big or small, are the building blocks of connection and joy.

Here's a story for you: Summer had a playdate with a friend, so Ollie stayed home with me. I figured having just one child to look after would be easier. I was wrong.

I tried to squeeze in some writing time while Ollie ate lunch, when he looked up and said, 'Mum, please can you play with me?' I'll be honest, my first thought was, 'Oh really?' I was tired and had a to-do list a mile long. But what came out of my mouth was, 'Sure, bub. What do you want to do?'

He chose hide-and-seek. We played a few rounds his way, and it got boring – fast. So, I thought, what if we played it Mum's way?

I queued up an absolute banger of a playlist, mainly to drown out the sound of his little feet tapping around the house, and then I was off. I slammed the back door to throw him off, then quickly ran the other way! Hide-and-seek suddenly felt so electric. I climbed trees, squeezed into cupboards (hoping I could get back out), and it was exhilarating – especially with old-school dance anthems pumping. And Ollie? He was having the time of his life.

This is just one glimpse of how shaking things up, playing your way, can completely shift your mood. In that moment, I sparked a wave of happiness, giving my body the biochemical boost it had been quietly craving. Later, as the day wound down, a lump rose in my throat – a mix of gratitude that I had said yes, and guilt that I nearly said no to my little boy. It reminded me how important it is to lean into those moments, to choose them even when it's easier not to. The proof was in how I felt: lighter, more alive, more present. That's when I realised I hold the power to change my negative emotions anytime, simply through fun. In that instant, the true value of these trigger tools became clear.

Nutritional biochemist Dr. Libby Weaver posed the question: 'Are we living too short and dying too long?' I thought – wow. As we get older, why does it sometimes feel like we already have one foot in the grave? We spend so much time thinking, planning, and overanalysing that we omit the part of life that actually requires us to live it.

I believe we're here to experience life. But when all we do is tick off to-do boxes, we disconnect from any real sense of meaning, of what it means to be human, and from living in a way that aligns with how our inner selves are quietly nudging us.

DOCTOR GOOGLE CAN'T FIX OUR FEELINGS

The digital age – love it or loathe it – has caused us to disconnect from the true nature of what it means to be human, and from what our minds and bodies need to function. Side note: There's nothing wrong with enjoying likes and comments on your social media, but it's not sustainable for long-term happiness. I'm not telling you something you don't already know here, but maybe the reiteration is helpful.

It's a complete waste of your time and money to follow the latest health fads, only to then sit on Instagram or TikTok feeling like a shallow version of yourself, because those platforms have wormed their way into your psyche and, in no uncertain terms, told you that you're not good enough. You're too fat, too skinny, too short, too tall. Your hips are too wide, you're too hairy, not hairy enough. Pimples, blotches, scars – and let's not forget the one toe that points east instead of north. Do this. Do that. Ping. Beep. Ding! It's nonstop noise pollution for your brain. Have you ever wondered after watching the news or scrolling on social media why you sometimes feel emotionally exhausted and drained?

SIDE NOTE

Also, I know most people mean well, and some just speak without thinking, but I think it's time we moved away from commenting on other people's physical appearance. I often get remarks about being short or having a small build, and honestly, it can still catch me off guard. You wouldn't walk up to someone and say they're fat, so why is it okay to say someone is too skinny, too short, or too tall?

When you hear those comments often enough, they start to chip away at you. The quiet message underneath is that you're not quite acceptable as you are. I have friends who hate being tall because it's always the first thing people mention about them. Unless it's said in a way that genuinely lifts someone up, maybe it's best we skip the physical assessments altogether.

It's been proven time and time again that the world we live in today is a completely different beast compared to when our parents were growing up – or even when you were a teenager. The challenges faced by today's teens and young families are on a whole other level.

'Well, ya know, it wasn't like that in my day...'

No, you're right, it wasn't. You were riding your bike without a helmet, your mum had no clue where you were, you drank from the garden hose, and your biggest worry was whether your mixtape would record off the radio without the DJ talking over it. Not to say there weren't real worries back then, of course, there were – but you're comparing apples with Bluetooth-enabled, AI-generated, anxiety-laden pears. It's just not the same.

THE GIFT-WRAPPED BEAST

Consumerism is also another beast we need to better understand. It tells us that to be happy, we must consume as many products and services as possible. We get a rush when we spot something we like, and a full-blown buzz when the package shows up at the door. Sure, we are happy – but like everything, it starts to wear thin. It's basically the knock-off version of happiness – looks good in photos, falls apart in real life after a while.

A cheap thrill in fancy packaging, pretending to be joy while quietly maxing out your account. So, when you think of consumerism, remember it triggers knock-off happy hormones.

What we need are real experiences – ones we can throw ourselves into and feel the benefits of for longer than bubble-gum takes to lose its flavour. Dancing in the kitchen or doing something fun with a friend lasts longer than the high from your new limited-edition trainers (and I love new trainers, so this is a harsh realisation for me). True joy comes from within, not just from placating our ego with another shiny delivery (though, let's be real, they smell nice and feel spongy).

Don't just take my word for it – try it the next time you experience real fun without consumerism, and see how long it lasts. Real joy creates a visceral reaction, one that runs deeper than the fleeting rush of surface-level pleasures.

As respected psychologist Tim Kasser says, 'Research shows that the more people value materialistic aspirations as goals, the lower their happiness and life satisfaction, and the fewer pleasant emotions they experience day to day.'

So many of us – including you – are becoming more aware of knock-off, fake dopamine fixes. They're not sustainable, and while we have a huge capacity to feel deeply and are built to do so, we're often fuelling ourselves with things that barely scratch the surface. It all starts to feel a bit … trivial. We are hungry for joy, only to be met with its used packaging.

So, what will it take for us to start prioritising the kind of happiness that lasts? Do we really have to hit rock bottom, fall apart, or face a serious diagnosis before we listen to what our hearts have been yearning for this whole time? As it was written in *The Alchemist*, you will never be able to escape your heart. So, it's better to listen to what it has to say.

WHAT MATTERS MOST

Bronnie Ware wrote a brilliant book called *The Top Five Regrets of the Dying*. Bronnie's book draws from her time as a palliative care nurse, where she spent years supporting people in their final days. Through these deeply personal experiences, she began to see clear patterns in the regrets people shared – on what they wished they had done differently in life.

The top five regrets of the dying: what they regretted most:

1. I wish I'd had the courage to live a life true to myself, not the life others expected of me.
2. I wish I hadn't worked so hard.
3. I wish I'd had the courage to express my feelings.
4. I wish I had stayed in touch with my friends.
5. I wish I had let myself be happier.

To be honest, my heart broke reading these, they carry a raw, undeniable honesty. I believe we're sent reminders like this to help us refocus on what truly matters. And number five really hits home with what we're talking about here. I'd often hear or read these insights, genuinely nod along, and then forget them just as quickly, usually because I glanced at the clock and realised I was late for school pick-up. That beautiful, soul-stirring thought? Gone. Replaced by to-do lists and daily noise.

Years from now, most of the stuff we stress about every day won't matter at all. If we got a do-over, most of us would probably make different choices. Right now, a lot of us just … know there's more out there – joy hiding in the corners we keep overlooking.

As Oprah says, 'The most important thing you can give yourself is your time.'

We all need something that yanks us out of our own heads for a while. There's no need to quit your job, ruin your marriage, run off to Bali, or shave your head to find it. This isn't a crisis; it's a recharge - something small that lights you up and reminds your brain it's allowed to have fun. And the best part? When you do that thing, your brain actually rewards you with happy chemicals. Real, felt joy, no drama required.

PERMISSION TO FEEL, GRANTED

It's hard to deny that many of us are tightly wound – shackled by responsibility, stressed, distracted, overlooked, frustrated, and at times, even hopeless. Some might go so far as to call it a toxic culture that we live in. We live the lives expected of us, and if we're being honest, most of us feel like something's missing. We do more for others than we do for ourselves, because that's how society has conditioned us to think. We're told it's selfish – even shameful – to prioritise our own health and well-being over the needs of those around us. But whether you hear it from me or someone else, here's the truth: that way of thinking is a one-way ticket to nowhere.

It's hard to start shifting our way of thinking. No one wakes up thinking, 'Gee, I hope someone pushes me out of my comfort zone today.' We like our comfort zones. They're … well, comfortable. I'm not here to flip your life upside down. I just want to offer a different perspective. Because even if you've got the basics down, a decent diet and regular exercise, there still might be something missing. And no, it's not more protein powder.

Sometimes, life is … fine. All things considered; you're doing okay. But deep down, you might feel like you're not really living the way you want to. Maybe you can't remember the last time you had a proper belly laugh or felt genuinely excited about something. When was the last time you did something spontaneous – just for the heck of it? So, I'll ask you: are you actively seeking out things that fill your cup? The routine of life is bittersweet. On the one hand, it helps us stay organised and efficient, which is great. But too much routine, and we risk becoming robots, just ticking off tasks while our deeper values, what really matters, go unchecked.

A Buddhist monk, Ajahn Sucitto, once said: 'Chaos may rattle you, but order can kill you.' There's wisdom in that tension. We need a little chaos now and then to remind us we're alive.

The most important element of this book isn't just to tell you to find a fun activity and go do it. It's to show you what can potentially happen to your health if you don't learn how to break out of a constant state of stress and mental fatigue. Emotional suffering can wreak havoc on our health in every way – and, as Peter Attia highlights in his book *Outlive*, many chronic illnesses begin developing far earlier than we realise. The problem is, we're too focused on treating symptoms once they appear, instead of preventing them in the first place. 'We are coming at this all too late,' he warns. Learning how to trigger your happiness through fun activities won't solve every problem, but it can solve a big one. As for the rest of the health tips and longevity hacks? I'll leave those to the experts.

REDEFINING FUN AS AN ADULT

That recreational fun in adulthood – especially the kind that sparks joy, laughter, and a sense of contentment – is one of the most undervalued resources in today's world? No matter what you do for work or what your family life looks like, playful fun is something entirely separate – something just for you. Yes, your job can be enjoyable. You might even be deeply passionate about it and feel lucky to do what you love. But here's the thing: it's still not light-hearted fun. I say this from experience – I fell into that exact trap. When your passion becomes your work, the 'off' switch disappears.

There's no true reset. Loving what you do and getting paid for it is a gift, absolutely. But it's not the kind of fun I'm talking about here.

Quick digression: I once saw author Elizabeth Gilbert speak live, and I loved what she said – that not everyone needs to love their job. If your job meets a basic need (money), and that money allows you to fund meaningful life experiences, then how wonderful is that? Do the nine-to-five. Don't bust your ass over it. Do just enough – and then give what's left to yourself and the people you love. Here's a wild idea: instead of pouring all your energy into a job you're not passionate about (especially when the benchmarks are unrealistic), invest that time and energy into fun. Into joy. Into you.

So, when did 'fun' become something only toddlers and Labradors are allowed to have? Somewhere along the line, we picked up this belief that being playful could make us look stupid, selfish, or like we've completely lost the plot.

And the go-to excuse? 'I just don't have time.' Right. We have time to scroll TikTok for forty-seven minutes in a blanket burrito, but no time to do something that actually sparks joy? Most of us have been quietly brainwashed by a society that says fun is not an effective use of our time. How dare you enjoy yourself and throw your errands to the wind! That's the voice of the over-functioning, guilt-ridden culture we've inherited. So, what did we do? We hit the mute button on joy. We shut down our impulses. And before we know it, we've become a glorified Wi-Fi signal – always connected, never really present. Just another slightly tired avatar in the digital matrix, wondering why we feel so flat.

DID YOU KNOW?

We have a designated play system in our brains, and it's the primary engine for brain development? We know how, because it was one of the skills we harnessed first as children, and it comes so naturally to us. It is almost like the desire fell away from us because we stopped doing it.

The two main reasons are straightforward. First, we may have forgotten how to switch on our fun mode regularly. Second, our inner critic (you know, that relentless little voice with a clipboard) won't shut up long enough to let us try.

Playful fun is kind of a big deal – but somehow, it's ended up on society's 'meh' list. It's powerful, it's joyful, and yet we treat it like a guilty pleasure instead of a basic human need. Here's the thing: play isn't some trendy self-care hack from a wellness influencer – it's ancient. Our fuzzy mammalian ancestors were tumbling around in the dirt, probably chasing each other for fun, throwing things at each other, and thriving on light-hearted chaos.

We didn't outgrow play – we just replaced it with emails and to-do lists. What a glow-up.

For some, it's hard to admit that we're trapped by our own thinking. We've settled into a kind of quiet complacency, going through the motions without even realising it. In the process, we've shut ourselves off – focusing on the mundane, the to-do lists, the mediocre tasks – while forgetting to look up and take in the world around us. We've become blind in our comfort, naïvely clinging to rose-coloured glasses that show us the world not as it is, but as we hope it to be – missing the real opportunities that are right in front of us.

Laughter isn't just a nice bonus when someone tells a good joke – it's a biological superpower. Science even says it: people who laugh regularly live longer, healthier lives.

And yet, most of us treat fun like a luxury. Why? Because we're stuck in survival mode, acting like the next disaster is lurking around every corner. But unless Scar from *The Lion King* is actually chasing you down your street, it's safe to step out of fight-or-flight for a minute.

We weren't built to live in constant fear. We were built to laugh, to connect, and yes, even to play. Laughter is self-care you can't overdose on.

THE INFLAMMATION WE NEED

We hear the word *inflammation* a lot, and it often gets a bad rap, but in the right context, it's pretty amazing. It's your body's built-in alarm system, designed to protect you when something's wrong, like an infection or injury. Short-term inflammation? Super helpful. But when it lingers, turning into chronic inflammation, that's when it becomes a problem. Dr. Peter Attia explains that this persistent, low-grade inflammation can damage our blood vessels and plays a key role in the development of atherosclerosis. Over time, it sets the stage for serious conditions like Alzheimer's disease and dementia.

That's where laughter and play come in. They're not just 'nice-to-haves' – they're core to our health because of how powerfully they reset the stress response. Picture Shrek saying, 'That'll do, Donkey.' Exactly that vibe.

You know the kind of laugh where your whole body joins in – the wheezing, the tears streaming down your face, maybe even a snort or two, and the sounds you make are hilarious all on their own. Once, I sat near a guy on a plane who, I kid you not, sounded exactly like the human version of Muttley. (By the way, if you don't know who Muttley is, google him and listen to his laugh. It's fantastic!)

The Muttley guy was glued to something on his phone, and his laugh had me in stitches the whole flight. I've no idea what he was watching, but his laugh ended up being the highlight anyway. I wasn't laughing *at* him, I was laughing *with* him – I'd caught the bug, if you catch my drift. Laughter is seriously contagious, and honestly, one of the greatest healers on the planet. You've probably heard people say, 'I need to laugh more.' Well, I'm here to say, absolutely you do. It's pure magic – effervescent and life-giving (more on laughter later).

As wonderful as laughter is, though, there are still things standing in the way of us finding our fun. I want to touch on something that feels especially relevant right now – the use of recreational drugs as a way to trigger happiness.

HANGOVERS AND THE LIKE

I feel like this deserves a spot in the book – not to rain on anyone's party, but because it's worth talking about. These days, it's common to reach for something quick and artificial to spark happiness. But when we start leaning too heavily on those shortcuts – whether it's a drink, a pill, or whatever's floating around – we end up outsourcing our joy.

Let me be clear – this comes with zero judgement. I'm a wine lover too. I live in South Australia, which happens to be one of the most celebrated wine regions in the world. So, I get it.

I'm not a medical professional, and I'm not here to hand out blanket advice like it's confetti. Life is complex, and so are our relationships with the things that bring us comfort. What I can offer is what I've come to understand through research, honest reflection, and real conversations with people who are also navigating this space. It's not about perfection – it's about curiosity, awareness, and exploring healthier, longer-lasting ways to feel good.

When we reach for external happiness supplements, we often miss the magic that's already right in front of us: connection, music, movement, belly laughs, and those odd little moments that remind us what it feels like to be really alive. You know, the real stuff.

Instead of tuning in, we start tuning out. We drift a little. We lose the thread. And before we know it, we're standing at a party, deep in conversation with someone passionately explaining their sourdough starter journey, wondering how we got there, and why we feel so oddly disconnected from ourselves.

Over time, though, if we keep outsourcing joy, we can start to feel a bit ... fuzzy. Out of it. Like we're floating just a few inches outside of ourselves. So here's the gentle nudge:

Why are we running from ourselves? No judgement – just curiosity. What are we avoiding? What would it feel like to stay fully here, even if it's a little awkward or uncomfortable at first?

Some people might say, 'I'm not running, I'm just having fun.' Fair enough. But I'd challenge that a bit, because fun, real fun, doesn't need additives. Play is part of your design. Joy is wired into you. It might just need a little unearthing.

And no, this isn't some floaty woo-woo stuff. This is you, being fully alive. And that's the best kind of high there is.

'LET'S TALK HIGHS' - BRAIN HIGHS

A drug-induced high – whether it's from stimulants, alcohol, or whatever's floating around at a festival – basically hacks your brain's reward system. It blasts it with feel-good chemicals like dopamine, serotonin, and endorphins … way more than your brain would ever dish out on its own.

It's fast. It's intense. It's a shortcut.

Your brain's no fool, though. It catches on and says, 'Well, if you're outsourcing joy like this, I'll just stop making it myself.' So now you need more of the thing to get the same buzz, and without it? You crash. Hard. Like, snack-on-the-floor-in-your-pyjamas-watching-animal-rescue-videos hard. Cue the shame spiral: what did I say, what did I do? It's an awful feeling, almost like you were hijacked and then dropped back on your arse the next day.

THE REAL DEAL - NATURAL HIGHS

These come from doing stuff that makes you feel properly alive: belly-laughing with friends, letting music move you, fun exercise, or even doing something epic – like quad biking with your mates. You choose your tonic!

Your brain still gives you the good stuff – in just the right doses to build you up, not burn you out. And the best part? No crash, no withdrawals, no hijacking.

In short: a drug high is like taking out a massive emotional loan with terrible interest. A natural high is like earning emotional interest on something you've genuinely invested in.

One numbs you out.

The other plugs you back in.

And honestly? You just can't beat a natural high. No hangover, no regrets – and it gets better the more you practice it.

What if we really took playful fun seriously? Imagine what future generations would look like – more creative, more connected, and emotionally resilient. What if corporate life made play a mandatory part of the workday? We'd likely see happier teams, fewer burnouts, and a whole lot more innovation. And what if our world leaders led by example – showing their humanity through play? Maybe then, diplomacy would be less about ego and more about empathy.

Just imagine: if we all made happiness a priority, if we used tools like play to tap into joy and connection, we could start healing the world – one person at a time. And the best part? It starts with something as simple as choosing to lean into what lights you up.

We all have the power to change our state of mind, even in small ways. To trigger joy. To lean into play. To laugh like Muttley, dance like nobody's watching, and embrace the small, electric moments that remind us we're alive.

If we do that, if we take our joy seriously, the world changes – one smile, one belly laugh, one playful moment at a time. And that, my friends, is a revolution that starts within us.

CHAPTER THREE

OUR MAGNIFICENT BRAINS

Experience enhances the brain.
~ Daniel J. Siegel ~

Just a quick reiteration: you're all the person you'll be the day you die. You're never too old to have fun!

I want to point out, although I'm sure it is obvious, that no computer comes close to matching the depth and complexity of the human self. Sure, machines can crunch numbers, recognise faces, or even mimic conversation, but that's a far cry from what it means to be human. Our sense of self is shaped by a whole mix of things – memories, emotions, relationships, culture, intuition, and all the little moments that make up our lives. It's not just about thinking; it's about feeling, imagining, reflecting, and growing. Computers might be getting smarter, but they don't feel joy, wrestle with doubt, or dream about the future. They don't have a past that shapes them or a personal story they carry. At the end of the day, the human self is something deeply layered and alive in a way no machine can truly replicate.

TINY NEURONS, BIG GOSSIP

Are you ready for some science? This is where I back up all the fun, fluffy stuff with irrefutable, evidence-based proof. Finding a form of fun and engaging with it isn't just nice – it comes with powerful health benefits that are hard to ignore.

Dr. Peter Attia, one of the big names in the longevity world, reminds us just how wild the human brain really is: 'It makes up only about two percent of our body weight, yet somehow hogs twenty percent of our total energy.' That's right, our brain is basically a tiny diva demanding constant fuel.

Inside this compact command centre are around eighty-six billion neurons. And each of those can connect to thousands of others – anywhere from one thousand to ten thousand connections per neuron. That's a ridiculous number of tiny conversations happening every second in your head ... and you thought your group chats were busy.

These connections – called synapses – are where the real magic happens. They form a pulsing, shape-shifting web that handles everything from thoughts and emotions to memories and identity. It's this tangled, buzzing network that helps us interpret the world, build relationships, and make decisions, whether brilliant or questionable, that shape who we are.

Our mental states are basically run by a team of tiny, overachieving scientists in our heads – nerves, neurons, synapses, and a cocktail of brain chemicals like dopamine, oxytocin, serotonin, and endorphins. They're the real MVPs, working 24/7 to keep us from turning into a complete emotional soup.

Neurons are found throughout your entire body, with the highest concentration in your brain and spinal cord. Alongside nerves, your brain and spinal cord form the core of your nervous system – basically the body's communication superhighway.

AGING BRAINS: SLOW DOWN OR SHAKE UP?

Now, please don't shoot the messenger ... but apparently, our neurons start aging in our twenties. Yep – while we were out making wild fashion choices and eating instant noodles at midnight, our brains were already quietly slowing down.

The good news? There's brain-boosting 'juice' for that. All you need are the right ingredients: games, curiosity, learning new things, staying active, and connecting with others – basically, a mix of fun and effort, kind of like group therapy meets trivia night.

Israeli neuroscientist Shlomo Benartzi says our brains are a bit like muscles – they need regular workouts to stay in shape. The catch? As we get older, we tend to settle into routines, and our brains slip into autopilot. Less thinking, more coasting.

The fix isn't complicated. Your brain loves novelty. Feed it new experiences, ideas, and challenges, and it starts firing off new neural pathways like a boss. Even small shake-ups – taking a different route to work, learning a new skill, or having a conversation that surprises you – can wake things up.

The bonus? That little mental stretch often comes with a boost in mood and a quiet little hit of 'Hey, I did something today.' It doesn't take much, but it makes a big difference.

Right now, we don't really have solid treatments for neuro-degenerative diseases – not the kind that actually work once things have started to go downhill. In his book *Outlive*, Peter Attia talks about the idea of a 'slow death'– how these diseases can quietly take hold in the body years, even decades, before we notice anything's wrong.

That's why waiting isn't really an option. By the time symptoms show up, the damage is often already done. The smart move? Get ahead of it. Act now, while there's still time to tip the odds in your favour.

STRESS: FRENEMY OR FULL-ON VILLIAN?

According to author and researcher Dr. Joe Dispenza, 'the chemicals of stress dysregulate and downregulate our genes,' ultimately leading to disease. The saddest part? Most people think they're the exception: 'That won't happen to me. I'll stay active. I can handle my stress.' But none of us is immune. Sometimes it takes seeing a friend or family member go through it for reality to hit – but even then, we often believe we'll be the lucky ones.

Joe talks about this in his work: new research in epigenetics shows that it's not just your genes calling the shots – it's your environment that tells your genes what to do. And guess what plays a huge role in that? Your emotions.

How you feel and respond to the world around you can send signals to your genes. If you're in a good space – feeling connected, supported, relatively chill, your genes get the green light to do their job and make healthy proteins. But if you're constantly stressed, overwhelmed, or stuck in negativity, those same genes might start making weaker, less healthy proteins. Over time, that can open the door to illness. Turns out your mood might be more powerful than you think.

PLAY: NOT JUST FOR KIDS

Our minds work a lot like computers – always processing, analysing, and sorting through endless streams of information. But unlike machines, we need more than just input – we need feeling. And often, what's missing is a little spark … a spark of joy, perhaps. That's where play comes in. It's not just for fun – it's a powerful tool for healing. Play can soothe trauma, ease loneliness, and serve as a much-needed remedy for the unpredictable twists and turns of life.

Play also does something surprising: it helps calm your immune system. When we're dealing with constant stress (not from viruses or shopping trolley germs, but from emotional stuff like rejection, loneliness, shame, or anxiety), our bodies react like we're under serious threat.

They go into full defence mode, pumping out these things called proinflammatory cytokines – basically, little immune warriors that are great at fighting real infections but not so helpful when you're just feeling overwhelmed. The result? Your body heats up, you feel foggy, tired, maybe even achy. That's your system stuck in fight mode over something emotional, not physical.

And that's where play comes in – it tells your body, 'Hey, we're safe now,' and helps dial that stress response way down.

Here's the problem: our minds can't always tell the difference between a physical threat and an emotional one. Therefore we end up with high cytokine levels just from stress and emotional strain, and if that's happening regularly, it takes a serious toll.

It's not all doom and gloom. There's a powerful, natural antidote that doesn't come in a pill bottle: play. But not just any play – your kind of play. The type that lights you up. Because if it's not fun, your dopamine levels won't rise, and you won't get the full mental and physical benefits.

SUBCONSCIOUS BRAIN: THE TESLA ON AUTOPILOT

Joe Dispenza says, 'Where you place your attention is where you place your energy.' And get this – only five percent of who we are operates from our conscious mind. The other ninety-five percent? That's all subconsciouses. When I first learned that it absolutely blew my mind. That ninety-five percent is made up of patterns and programs we've memorised over time – habits, beliefs, emotional reactions, social conditioning – all running quietly in the background. And as Danish author Tor Nørretranders puts it, 'The subconscious brain is a thousand times more powerful than the conscious mind.' Hmmm … our autopilot is driving the Tesla way more often than we think.

The real remedy is action. Don't just tell yourself you're fine – show your body you are. Trigger those feel-good biochemicals through play, laughter, movement, and joy. Don't wait for stress to take over; shift your state.

Because when you're stressed, your brain shifts into a psychological state that affects everything. Remember the 'switch flicking' we talked about in Chapter 1? Under stress, your prefrontal cortex – the part that handles rational thinking – gets hijacked. The amygdala steps in, flipping you into fight-or-flight mode. It's like a sudden gear shift, and that's why thinking clearly or making good decisions can feel nearly impossible in those moments.

I've had times where I was so stressed, I was literally bouncing off things in the kitchen – trying to get stuff done but failing at everything I touched – which made me feel even shittier. Now I get why. Or maybe you've found yourself snapping at your family or coworkers and shouting, 'Ahh, I just can't think straight!' Yep. That's not you losing it – that's your brain doing exactly what it's wired to do under pressure.

Stress and emotions are closely linked – they come from the same part of the brain. When we feel stressed, it's usually because the brain is getting us ready to act. It sends out cortisol, a hormone designed to get us moving. That's followed by a burst of energy, as glucose is released into the bloodstream. Your heart, lungs, and muscles all kick into gear, preparing your body to deal with whatever's coming – even if that threat is purely psychological.

The problem is, many of us are stuck in this stressed state way more often than we should be. That's why learning how to tap out of it – by actively triggering joy – is one of the most effective ways to reset your brain and regain control. Laughter can do this immediately for us.

THE JOYFUL SCIENCE OF LAUGHTER AND MOVEMENT

Stress can actually be thrilling – and even a little addictive. Think about riding a roller coaster. You strap yourself in, your heart races, and you're filled with nerves and excitement, but you chose to be there, and that makes all the difference. It's that rush of anticipation; we're tapping the adrenaline pedal just enough to feel alive. The best part? We're in control. We like our stress with a side of fun, just enough to keep things exciting without feeling overwhelmed.

Also, fuck getting on a roller coaster now. Maybe when I was fifteen – but these days, I'll choose something more suited to me, rather than feeling like my insides are trying to escape my body.

Stress, in the short term – and when used wisely – can actually be pretty helpful. A little stress gives you a shot of adrenaline, which can help your body fight off infections and even boost your immune system.

The trick? Give your body what it needs after the stress has done its job: rest, a good meal, maybe a nap. Stress can help us perform better, think sharply, and even show up stronger. It adds value to our lives ... just not in unlimited servings.

Like cake, or wine, or group chats that never end – too much of a good thing, and you're begging for mercy.

Think of fun as food for your brain. Playing provides nutrients that help stimulate nerve growth, which means we might just dodge some of those pesky neurological problems later in life. It's like doing squats for your neurons. On the flip side, stress hormones like cortisol, epinephrine, and norepinephrine show up like the party crashers they are – slamming the brakes on blood flow and tanking your nitric oxide levels. Translation? You start feeling blah, unmotivated, maybe even a little like a sad potato.

Stress also plays a big role in how well you retain memories and learn new skills. But when stress takes over? Yikes. Your libido drops, your immune system slows down like it's on vacation, and suddenly bam! Weight gain, rising cholesterol, and heart issues start creeping in.

I remember my friend Adriana sending me a text after she volunteered at the school colour run. Basically, the kids wear white, run around the oval in a circle, and the parents and teachers throw powdered paint on them – just for fun. The kids had clearly had enough, but Adriana caught the wave of excitement and wasn't done yet. She glanced at what she had left and decided to cover the mums next to her. It took them a microsecond to join in and do the same. Adriana took a picture, sent it to me, and said, 'You're right about this play stuff – it's so much fun, I needed that release'.

To be clear, we're talking about long-term stress – and our general lack of understanding about how to shift ourselves out of that state of mind. Our brains are wired for fun. It keeps our bodies healthier and our minds more creative. So, be silly, dance around, chase your dog, play a game. Your neurons will thank you, and your stress hormones won't know what hit them.

NEUROCHEMICAL MVPs: DOPAMINE, OXYTOCIN & CO.

Playing as adults builds brain connections – and that's where the biggest growth happens. It's not about the win or the result; it's about the fun. Fun is the secret sauce your brain is hunting for when you play. Developmental psychologist Gordon Neufeld nailed it: 'We used to think schools built brains, but it's actually play that does; it's where the most growth happens.' Can we get a hallelujah? Because that's some statement!

Gordon puts it best: 'If adults make regular play part of their lives, it boosts intelligence and productivity, toughens up our resilience, and helps us manage our emotions.' In other words, play makes you smarter, calmer, and better at not flipping your desk over. And we're not just talking crossword puzzles here. When you play regularly, the parts of your brain responsible for focus, attention, emotional regulation, and creativity get a solid upgrade. It's like giving your prefrontal cortex a spa day and a personal trainer at the same time.

So next time your slave-driver boss demands more without a break, just flash a serene smile and say: 'I'm not slacking – I'm playing to become more neurologically efficient.'

Then spin slowly in your chair like a majestic dolphin. Bonus points if you make gentle sonar noises.

And here's the best part: your brain loves this. Play triggers a four-hormone symphony – dopamine, serotonin, oxytocin, and endorphins. These aren't just feel-good chemicals; they're the VIPs of motivation, connection, and mental health.

Dopamine is your internal hype coach, pushing you toward goals and rewarding you when you get there. Low enthusiasm for a task?

That's your dopamine saying, 'Hey, maybe this spreadsheet isn't your soul's purpose.' So yes, play is fun – but it's also powerful, neurological self-care. That's a beautiful thing.

IF YOU DON'T USE IT, YOU LOSE IT

We know how beneficial it is for young children, but as adults, we can struggle to reach our play states as easily as children do. The scientific reason is that children aren't ruled by their prefrontal cortex and can insert themselves into the fun. My thought is they don't have a doom list or responsibilities, so they can play all damn day. They aren't looking after elderly parents, and they sure as hell aren't looking after themselves. More on how to find the time comes in the 'Clock Yourself' chapter.

Playing as adults is a marvellous quick fix for our aging brains. Research shows that our beloved dopamine is closely tied to curiosity. When we follow our curiosity and satisfy it, we trigger a biochemical joy bomb that lights us up from the inside. There's a reason your brain starts looking like Guy Fawkes Night – it's having the time of its life! And the best part? You made that happen.

As we age, it can feel like a slippery slope – that's where the old saying 'you can't teach an old dog new tricks' comes from. People tend to give up on themselves. But it's not that we can't learn new things. It's that these playful, engaging activities are more important than ever as we age. Another saying? 'If you don't use it, you lose it.' And it turns out that one's got some serious truth behind it.

As we get older, learning something new can feel like a challenge. Multi-tasking gets tricky, names and numbers slip through the cracks, and suddenly you're calling the place saying, 'I'm so sorry I missed my appointment – I completely forgot!' Some studies show that about a third of older adults struggle with declarative memory (that's the memory used for facts and events). But here's the twist – other studies reveal that one in five seventy-year-olds perform just as well on cognitive tests as people in their twenties. Food for thought, hey?

When you play as an adult, you have the wonderful perspective to appreciate what brings you joy, and you can create something with yourself, using your mind and your body. These activities help grow the parts of the brain that handle memory, emotions, and behaviour. Doing fun activities that challenge your brain can improve how it works and even help prevent memory issues. It also relieves stress, boosts creativity, and keeps your mind sharp. Plus, it helps you feel younger and more energised.

In 2050, the predicted number of people living with Alzheimer's in America is thirteen million. Health and long-term care costs for people living with dementia are projected to reach nearly $1 trillion in 2050. And did you know that our brain changes more than any other part of our bodies? Certain parts actually shrink, and the lifetime risk for Alzheimer's at age forty-five is one in five women and one in ten men. When you isolate yourself, the risk of developing dementia is about fifty percent higher.

According to the brilliant author and physician Dr. Gabor Maté, 'Neural exercises such as play provide resilience and help us regulate our emotional states.' He also points out that play is a powerful form of relaxation for adults. And the best part? There doesn't need to be any goal or purpose beyond simply having fun. No endgame, no outcome – just joy for the sake of joy. And that's more than enough.

Another beautiful and wise friend of mine, author and grief counsellor Kay Backhouse once told me she had no idea why she'd stopped playing the piano. She, too, found herself questioning, 'What's the point of doing this?' Then she had a lightbulb moment: 'I know why – because I enjoy it. And that's the only fucking reason I need.' She said it in her charming Yorkshire accent – I'm sure you can just imagine it.

VAGUS NERVE: THE PARTY PLANNER OF YOUR BODY

Have you heard of the vagus nerve – aka the vagal nerves? Sounds like a party, right? It's the tenth cranial nerve, and it runs from your brainstem down to your heart, lungs, and gut – basically the VIP of your nervous system, doing meet-and-greets with your most important organs. So yes, it's a nerve with one heck of a tour schedule.

Believe it or not, your gut and your vagus nerve are kind of the bossy ones in the relationship – they tell your brain what to do. While your brain thinks it's running the show, your gut-level instinct system and the vagal system are basically like, 'Hey up there, we've got a situation – do something!' So next time you get a gut feeling, just know it might actually be your vagus nerve gently (or not-so-gently) yelling, 'Get it together, brain!'

The vagus nerve is kind of the unsung hero of your nervous system. It's closely tied to feelings of happiness and well-being and plays a big role in calming your body down when life gets a bit … intense. When you do something that sparks joy – like laughing, connecting with someone, or dancing like no one's watching – you're giving your vagus nerve a little high-five. And when it's activated, magical things happen: your blood pressure drops, your stress response chills out, and inflammation takes a back seat. So basically triggering happiness = vagus nerve doing a happy dance = your whole body saying, 'Ahhh, thank you.'

HORMONE SYMPHONY

Also, did you know that the autonomic nervous system has two parts? The sympathetic and parasympathetic systems. They control the same body functions, but in opposite ways. The sympathetic system is your body's gas pedal – getting you ready for action (fight or flight). The parasympathetic system is the brake – helping you relax, rest, and digest. So, where does play come in? To put it simply, it achieves a balance in the nervous system's responses to stress and environmental demands. It's exactly what we need.

A snapshot of happy hormones:

- Dopamine – nailing tasks, self-care activities, eating well, listening to music, etc.
- Endorphin – exercising, laughing, socialising, dancing, singing, eating dark chocolate.
- Oxytocin – giving to others, deep and meaningful conversations, playing with pets, hugs, yoga, when my kids offer to brush my hair, OMG so relaxing. Or sniffing babies' heads (that may just be me, but if you know, you know).

FUN – done right – has the power to shape the brain and open your imagination to infinite possibilities. It invigorates the soul.

CHAPTER FOUR

HAHA!

Laugh first because it's the fastest way to feel better.
~ Shanelle Franklin ~

Laughter is basically the ultimate heart-opener, like a magical key that makes everything feel a little less crazy and a lot more refreshed. When your heart's flung wide open, suddenly people don't seem so estranged, the world gets lighter, and life feels way more doable. You know the kind of laugh I'm talking about – the bellyaching, can't-breathe, tears-streaming-down-your-face, 'Whoa, I really needed that!' kind of laugh. In those moments, you don't just feel happy – you feel like you've unlocked a secret level of joy, alive and totally connected. And here's the science party happening inside you: your body is throwing a wild cocktail bash with feel-good hormones all dancing through your bloodstream, lighting up your brain like it's in Ibiza. The result? A happiness explosion that no pill, potion, or magic smoothie can touch.

COMEDY WITH PURPOSE

Comedians often walk a fine line when making jokes about painful or dark topics. But the point of this kind of humour isn't to mock suffering – it's to create space for relief and reflection. When a comedian makes a joke about something tragic, they're not laughing at the victim or the event itself – that would be cruel and sadistic. Instead, they're inviting us to confront what's difficult through the lens of humour. They're saying: "This thing happened, and it was awful – but we can survive it. We can even laugh again.'

Humour has long been a coping mechanism. It helps us metabolise pain, release tension, and find our footing again after life throws us off balance. We don't need laughter just to celebrate joy – we need it to get through pain. If we only laugh when things are good, we miss out on one of humour's greatest gifts. We laugh to survive the hard parts. That's where laughter becomes medicine. It doesn't erase the pain, but it softens its edges.

On my podcast, *The Beautiful Nightmare*, Tamara and I chatted with comedian Georgie Carroll. She told us that whenever one of her friends is going through a really rough time – I'm talking life-is-testing-you, not stub-your-toe rough – she has a … unique way to cheer them up.

Georgie somehow sneaks into their house, hides in the pantry, and the second they walk in … she pops out naked. Just to make them laugh. Can you even imagine your best friend doing that? You'd be shocked, speechless, and also completely floored that someone thinks so highly of you that they'll straight-up strip to make you smile. Absolute legend.

NOT EVERYTHING IS A LAUGHING MATTER

Of course, not everyone is ready to laugh at everything – and that's okay. We all carry different wounds, and some are fresher than others. There are topics you might feel are too raw to find funny, and that's a personal boundary worth honouring – it is a healthy act of self-care. The key is understanding that humour, when used with care, isn't a sign of disrespect – it's often an invitation to process. And if something doesn't sit right with you, you don't have to engage with it.

Sometimes, we get angry at jokes on false pretences – not because the humour itself is cruel, but because we haven't yet come to terms with the underlying hurt. That's human. But instead of silencing laughter altogether, maybe we can get curious about why it struck a nerve. Because laughter, even in the darkest places, can be a step toward healing – a sign that something in us still wants to feel joy, even when life's been hard.

HONOUR YOUR FUNNY BONE

I'm instantly devastated whenever I hear someone say, 'Oh no, I don't like my laugh,' like they're trying to pull back that glorious sound that escaped exactly the way it was meant to. Kids? They don't care one bit how they sound. The crazier you are, the more they show you how much they appreciate your willingness to embrace silliness. Somewhere along the way – and trust me, I'm watching my own kids closely to see when this sneaky self-doubt creeps in – kids start losing that carefree spirit. My nine-year-old daughter has already begun to soften that unapologetic freedom to be herself – that fearless, no-judgement way of just being. I think for most kids it hits around the pre-teen years, when the 'Better not be myself or I might get rejected – I have to fit in' self-talk takes centre stage.

My laugh? It's loud, brash, and when I really get going, it sounds like all the air is being concertinaed out of me. It sometimes turns heads, but honestly, I can't help it – I just let it rip! Even my three-year-old niece mimics my laugh in her cheeky attempt to take the piss out of me. Watching her makes me laugh even more – maybe that's her secret plan! The point is: laughter should never be filtered or stifled – unless, of course, it's hurting someone's feelings. In that case, I say stop immediately. Bullying and making someone the butt of jokes? Totally awful. Remember this: we shouldn't pump up our own tyres by letting someone else's down. I have a hunch, though, that you're not that kind of person anyway.

KIDS AS OUR LAUGHTER TEACHERS

Laughter is basically the original 'reset button' humans have been using since forever. Think of it as life's way of saying, 'Whoa, slow down – let's hit pause and have some fun.' Babies? They're like tiny, unstoppable laugh machines, giggling their little faces off before they can even say 'mama' or 'why?' These mini comedy clubs laugh somewhere between 300 and 400 times a day. Meanwhile, adults are out here looking like the sad, serious versions of ourselves, managing maybe fifteen to twenty chuckles a day if we're lucky – and that's on a good day. Stressful day? Scratch that. You might get one or two half-hearted snorts before coffee.

Honestly, when was the last time you had a proper, can't-breathe, tears-rolling-down-your-face laugh? If it's hard to remember, that's okay – but it shows you need it. That quiet little 'Where did all the fun go?' feeling. If laughter were a bank account, a lot of adults would be overdrawn – running on empty and quietly craving a top-up.

So, maybe it's time to take a page out of toddler town and unleash those laughs like confetti at a party. If kids can laugh 300 times a day, surely we grown-ups can manage at least fifty without feeling like we're embarrassing ourselves. Because let's be real – laughter is the oldest, coolest circuit breaker we have. It zaps stress, flips our mood from 'meh' to 'boom,' and gives our brain a fireworks show that New Year's parties around the world would envy.

MARY POPPINS AND FLOATING FUN

Remember that scene in *Mary Poppins* where Uncle Albert laughs so hard he floats to the ceiling? Classic Disney magic – but also sneakily deep.

The message? Joy lifts you – literally and emotionally. Laughter isn't just fun; it's freeing. When you stop taking life so seriously, you rise above the grind (and maybe your furniture).

And the jokes? Terrible on purpose. Because it's not about being clever – it's about letting go. Even the stiffest grown-ups (yes, Mary, we're looking at you) could use a little float time. Also, I love Mary so much, I wish she lived in my house.

Bonus meaning: feelings are contagious. Once one person lightens up, others follow. But when the mood shifts? Boom – everyone's back on the floor. Proof that joy is precious … and fleeting.

Moral of the story? Laugh more. Float often. And don't wait for a flying nanny to remind you.

Throw yourself into anything that sparks laughter – seriously, watch videos of pandas tumbling off things or dogs trying to fit into boxes way too small for them. Pure gold. Call that one friend who always makes you laugh until you cry. And if you don't have someone like that in your life right now, don't stress – that's where your sense of play comes in. You've got to put yourself out there a little. Join a pickleball team, hit up a comedy club, try something random like a laughter yoga class (yes, it's a thing – and yes, it's as crazy and fun as it sounds).

The key is to get out of the 'I can't, I won't, I don't' mindset – because if you stay there, nothing changes. You've got to grab the wheel and steer toward the stuff that lights you up and also shakes that routine a little. Curiosity is your secret weapon here. Let it guide you to the next moment that makes you laugh so hard you forget why you were stressed in the first place.

LAUGHTER AS A COPING MECHANISM

I hate to admit this – but sometimes (okay, fine, often) I laugh when I'm not supposed to. Sometimes when I hear sad news. Or when my husband Dan – or one of my kids – trips over something. I know, I'm awful. Dan usually just sighs and says, 'Oh, there you go again – I knew you'd do that,' while staying calm and caring, like a proper grown-up. Meanwhile, I'm doubled over, tears streaming, racing to the nearest toilet because I've completely lost it – and so has my pelvic floor.

But here's the thing: there's actually a scientific explanation for this (which I now tell Dan regularly as my official Get-Out-of-Guilt card). It turns out that laughing in sad or awkward situations is a legit coping mechanism. The brain uses it to manage emotional overload. It's like a pressure release valve – when things feel too heavy, laughter steps in to keep us from falling apart. And since the areas of the brain that handle laughing and crying are right next to each other, the lines can get blurry when emotions are running high.

SCHADENFREUDE: THE GUILTY GIGGLE

Have you heard of the word *schadenfreude*? It's a fancy German word that means 'finding joy in someone else's misfortune.' Yes, it sounds a little wicked – but hang on, it's not always as villainous as it seems.

It's that tiny spark of glee when:
- The office know-it-all's printer jams mid-brag.
- Your sibling gets caught sneaking snacks after telling on you for doing the same thing.
- Someone struts confidently onto a dance floor ... and immediately wipes out.
- Your egocentric boss walks into a glass door.

We're not bad people – we're just human. Schadenfreude is like life's little emotional loophole: we're not laughing at someone's pain, we're laughing because we relate, or because karma finally showed up in Crocs. And people also look and sound funny in those moments.

And here's the sweet part: often, schadenfreude is more about relief than cruelty. A subconscious, 'Phew, that could've been me.' Or even a light-hearted way we bond over life's embarrassing, messy, and wonderfully humbling moments.

So, if you've ever laughed at a fail video, or snorted when your friend slipped over (and then you immediately asked if they were okay – mid-giggle) – you, dear heart, have experienced schadenfreude. No shame. Just a little giggle from the soul ... with love.

Now, I do realise I said earlier that we shouldn't laugh at other people's expense – and I stand by that. But let's be real: there's a big difference between bullying someone and bursting into laughter when your six-foot-tall husband hardcore trips over his own feet on his way out of the pantry … after sneakily raiding the kid's lunchbox snacks. You get it, I'm sure.

Think of laughter as the brain's quick little escape hatch when it needs it. A way to reframe pain, connect with others, and remind us that even in the messiest moments, there's room for absurdity, and a reason to smile – even if it's wildly inappropriate, like during a quiet yoga class or at church. Especially if someone accidentally lets out a cheeky fluff. Farts are funny. Gross, but funny.

Laughter has a way of making problems seem smaller. It lifts the weight from our shoulders with humour and ease. A couple of years ago, at my Granny's dying bedside in the hospital, two kinds of tears were flowing: one tied to grief, the other to laughter. I was sitting with my extended family, and we were laughing – not just giggling, but snorting, wheezing, gasping-for-air kind of laughing. Tears rolled down our faces as we shared impersonations, old stories, and the to-do list my Gran had left us – heck, she was funny. Some might have called it insensitive, but my Gran was a Scottish lady who loved to laugh. People can often confuse a Scottish wake for a birthday party because laughter, for us, is a way of coping. We were loud, and it was late. My mum, half-laughing and half-crying, said, 'The nurses will think we're horrible – laughing at a time like this. Poke your head out the door and apologise.' (Oh yes, I'll be the scapegoat for us.) When I opened that door, what I found was truly magical. At the nurses' station, I was met not with scowls, but with smiles and quiet affirmation. One of the nurses said, 'Please don't stop that sound. I can't tell you how long it's been since I've heard laughter like that on this ward.' It turned out our laughter had become energy. It carried through the hospital door and filtered down the ward. Other patients, who didn't know what we were laughing about, had started laughing too – at nothing more than the sound of joy.

LAUGHING IS CONTAGIOUS

When you witness someone laughing, there's an energetic glow that radiates – it's magnetic. Like the story I shared earlier about the Muttley guy on the plane – his laugh was so infectious that even the woman sitting in front of him turned around to catch someone's eye. Lucky for me, it was mine. In that moment, we shared a little energy exchange over how brilliantly joyful his laughter was. Who was she? I have no idea. And the best part is – I didn't need to know. The magic was in that momentary connection, sparked by something as simple and pure as laughter. It bonded two strangers. We smiled, gave a little giggle, and that was it. And the lingering effect it had on my mental state for the rest of that flight was exactly what I needed after a full-on weekend of work.

If 'Muttley Man' hadn't been laughing so freely, I'm certain that warm, three-second burst of shared joy wouldn't have happened. We were both in sheer admiration of him – just being himself, sounding absolutely brilliant, and unknowingly making everyone around him feel lighter. His happiness made us feel happy too.

Three strangers, connected by a sound – each of us having triggered that beautiful biochemical response inside, thanks to the simplest, most human thing: laughter.

THE SCIENCE OF LOL (Laugh Out Loud)

Leaning into the things that trigger our laughter can quite literally flick the 'stress switch' back to the off position. Remember, stress is your body shifting from one state to another – it's a survival mechanism. But when you laugh, you signal to your body that you're safe. Your amygdala, the part of your brain responsible for detecting threats, gets the memo and can finally relax. After all, it doesn't need to gear you up for danger when you've suddenly stopped in your tracks to laugh until you can't breathe.

Laughter really is a powerful antidote to stress. And if you'd like a visual – think of your stresses as a cauldron bubbling over with every shitty, stressy thing thrown in. Think of laughter as a way to rebalance its pH levels – it doesn't erase the mess, but it neutralises the burn.

It's important not to shame people for inviting laughter when tensions are running high – again, not to mock someone or a situation, but to release the tension. We don't look strong or noble when we shame people – we stay stuck. We lose connection, we lose release, and we lose a chance to heal.

Let's be honest: we're all walking around with a bubbling cauldron inside us. Not the cute kind that comes with sparkles and spells, but the kind that's constantly simmering with stress, overwhelm, and the occasional leftover grudge from three years ago. It's there, quietly hissing away in the background while we smile politely, pay bills, reply to messages with 'no worries!' (even though there are worries) and try to act like we've totally got this.

Spoiler alert: most of us don't totally have this. And that's the point – we aren't meant to.

CHAPTER FIVE

WHAT'S IN YOUR CAULDRON?

Double, double toil and trouble; fire burn and cauldron bubble.
~ William Shakespeare, Macbeth ~

The ingredients vary, but here are some common ones:
- A sprinkle of sleep deprivation
- A generous dollop of work deadlines
- A handful of school drop-offs, forgotten lunchboxes, and costume days that weren't on the calendar
- A blob of financial tension
- A cup of shame
- A splash of relationship friction
- A hint of being needed too much
- A pinch of 'I should be doing more' guilt
- A sizeable amount of wearing the stressors of the people around you (hello, empaths)
- A teaspoon of loneliness
- A tablespoon of 'I'm not enough'

And if you're lucky, you'll get the bonus ingredient: unexpected emotional chaos. You know the kind – tearing up at a reel someone sent you, or flying into a wildly disproportionate rage because someone used your special mug or spoon. Or, in my case, getting into a slightly-too-intense debate with Dan about the word *'floordrobe.'* He insists the floor is a perfectly valid storage solution for clothes that are too dirty for the wardrobe but too clean for the wash basket.

I let him win this one. We compromised, and he has his own corner. He's happy, the clothes are somewhere he can see them, and I stopped adding them to my cauldron of stress.

Your cauldron doesn't ask for permission. It just collects things – little things, big things, things you didn't even know were bothering you…

Until they bubble back up mid-argument like:

'AND ANOTHER THING!'

(Surprise! You were still mad about that thing from three months ago.)

THE BOIL-OVER MOMENT

We all have them. The moment the cauldron spills over. Maybe it's a shout. A tear. A door slammed harder than it needed to be. Or a spontaneous meltdown in the middle of Woolies because they've moved the avocados. Again. Or sold out of your favourite oat or almond milk.

These aren't moments of weakness. They are signs that your internal stress brew has reached maximum capacity. The pressure's too much, and your body and brain are just trying to let a little steam out before you explode.

ENTER: LAUGHTER (AKA YOUR MAGICAL ANTIDOTE)

Here's where laughter becomes your secret weapon. It's not just a reaction to something funny – it's your nervous system saying, 'Oh thank God, we're not dying after all.' Laughter sends a direct message to your amygdala (that ancient part of your brain responsible for detecting danger) and says, 'You can relax now. We're safe. We're okay.'

It's like adding a calming ingredient to your stress smoothie. Something fizzy, sparkly, and wonderfully absurd. And while it doesn't remove the stressors completely (sadly, the tax deadline doesn't disappear with a chuckle), it does neutralise their grip on you. It brings the boiling point down.

REAL-LIFE PROOF: MUTTLEY MAN

Take my recent flight, for example. I'd just wrapped a full-on weekend of work, mentally and physically drained. I was on the mic for hours on end, and my energy levels had plummeted on my way home. So, I'm on a plane, quietly stewing in my own cauldron of stress, when I hear it – this unfiltered, wheezy, snickering snort – like a mischievous giggle that got stuck in his throat. Pure, unselfconscious hilarity.

It was so contagious – and just like that, a total stranger's laugh lightened the emotional load I didn't even realise I'd been dragging around. My cauldron stopped bubbling for a moment. I could breathe. I smiled for the rest of that flight. And I'm not exaggerating when I say it changed the rest of my day.

STIRRING THE POT (IN A GOOD WAY)

Laughter won't fix everything. But it softens things. It gives your nervous system a break, your perspective a shift, and your mood a nudge in the right direction.

So, what do we do with this magical ingredient? We lean into it. We actively seek it out. Watch videos of goats on trampolines. Call that one friend who makes you cry laughing. Go to a comedy show. Play with kids. Be daft. Let yourself be ridiculous.

Your cauldron needs balancing. Regularly. And laughter is one of the best, fastest, and most natural ways to stir the pot without letting it boil over.

You don't need to earn your laughter. You don't have to wait until everything's calm, perfect, or 'dealt with.' Laughter doesn't mean you're not taking life seriously – it means you're giving yourself a break from taking everything so damn seriously all the time.

So next time you feel the heat rising, ask yourself: *What can I toss into this bubbling mess to lighten it?* And if the answer is laughter – well, you're already halfway to feeling better.

Let's recap:

1. **THROW IN A GIGGLE GRENADE (AKA WATCH SOMETHING RIDICULOUS)**

   When the stress mess starts simmering, hit pause and inject it with something that makes you laugh. Think pandas falling out of trees, dogs wearing sunglasses, or a stand-up special where the comedian laughs at their own jokes. Laughter is your emotional bicarbonate soda – it fizzes, settles, and neutralises the acidity of your day.

   Bonus tip: Watch something you've already seen and loved. The anticipation of your favourite funny moment doubles the joy!

   Dan and I will often lie in bed and watch videos of a comedian called Jethro before going to sleep if we need a laugh.

2. **CALL YOUR CHAOS FRIEND**

   You know that one person who finds the absurd in everything and turns every phone call into a therapy session disguised as banter? Call them. Text them. FaceTime them while sitting in your car, eating chips. You don't need deep advice – you need them to say, 'You did what? That's mental – I love it.' Boom. Cauldron stirred.

   Sometimes I call my sister, and the second she picks up, I say something completely unhinged. Or I make weird noises. Or I just hold the phone up to the TV and play clips from the movies we grew up on and laughed at – *Corrina, Corrina, Dumb and Dumber, Billy Madison,* you name it. It's completely ridiculous, but she laughs hard. Box ticked. Her sense of humour is as warped as mine, so it works.

Even one of the event providers I MC for picks up the phone and says, 'Here she is, my favourite fucking moll!' – and then can't catch her breath from laughing before I can even say a word back.

So, call your chaos friend when you need to tap out of your emotional overload. Don't have a chaos pal? Time to audition some (more on this in a later chapter).

3. MOVE (AND WHO CARES WHAT ANYONE THINKS)

Pop on your favourite playlist and just start moving. Dance, strut, shimmy, flail – whatever feels good. Go full Beyoncé if you're feeling it, or channel a printer trying to shake off a paper jam: random angles, weird pauses, zero rhythm, one hundred percent heart. It's strangely impressive and slightly chaotic. I've stopped caring when my kids witness the monstrosity that is me on the kitchen dance floor. In fact, I sometimes plan it for when they walk in – their faces are priceless. Their reactions scream that they are embarrassed for me. And if I can hold it together long enough, I'll keep going. Just for the drama.

The goal isn't to look cool – it's to shake out the tension, wake up your endorphins, and sneak a little silliness into your system. Your body (and your mood) will be grateful.

PHYSICAL MOVEMENT + RIDICULOUSNESS
=
EMOTIONAL RESET

4. SAY IT OUT LOUD (EVEN IF IT'S JUST TO THE DOG)

Sometimes the pot simmers because you've said nothing. You're bottling, swallowing, steam-building. So say it. Rant to the wall. Vent to your pet. Narrate your meltdown like

David Attenborough. You'll feel ridiculous, which is perfect – that's laughter's cue to slide in.

Dogs are excellent listeners. Cats, less so; they may just walk off. Of course, if you are a cat lover, you'll argue with me on this. Thank you to my dog, Charli for listening to all my relentless rants.

5. DO SOMETHING POINTLESSLY FUN

Paint something badly. Play handball. Eat cereal out of a mixing bowl. Sit in your car and just sing (I highly recommend Diana Ross and Lionel Richie's *Endless Love* – it's a cracker for that). Or maybe you're Slash the guitarist for a hot minute!

My daughter Summer has a routine: 'Right, Mum, make me laugh.' She fills her mouth with water, cheeks puffed, just waiting for the moment. And I attempt to deliver.

Once, I heard my friend Cassie's son blurt out a word I'll never forget: *Disgusta-Bum*. It's what he calls someone who's upset him. Brilliant. Completely disarming in any heightened situation. I have no doubt he will deny using this word when he is a teenager. Call your slavedriver boss a *Disgusta-Bum* – not to their face, obviously, but maybe to your favourite co-worker who gets you. You'll feel fantastic.

So, I'll blurt out 'DISGUSTA-BUM!' at full volume, and nine times out of ten, the water goes everywhere. Summer chokes a little but laughs even harder. Mission accomplished.

We get so caught up in being productive that we forget how powerful pointless fun can be. It's not immature – it's preventative medicine for your inner adult meltdown.

Reminder: Not everything has to have a purpose. Joy counts.

Sometimes your cauldron doesn't need new ingredients – it just needs you to turn down the heat. Rest. Nap. Say no. Cancel things. That's not weakness; that's smart kitchen management.

I've only recently learned this one. The first time I properly flexed my 'no' muscle, it was oddly lifechanging. For a lifelong people-pleaser, it felt impossible at first – but once you do it, it's electrifying. Saying no to protect your energy isn't rude or selfish; it's responsible cauldron care. You're not rejecting others – you're accepting yourself.

And while we're stirring the pot, let's talk about one of the biggest blockers to laughter: loneliness. Not just the 'haven't texted a friend all day' kind, but the quiet, creeping kind that can follow you even in a crowd. Chronic loneliness is serious - it can actually shorten your life by up to fifteen years.

Think of your nervous system as a little boat at sea. In our tribal days, we paddled together. Now, too many of us drift alone, trying to stay afloat. That's when laughter becomes your flare gun – it signals connection, warmth, and safety. Even for a moment, it reminds your brain: *I'm not alone in this boat.*

But laughter isn't just good for the soul – it's surprisingly good for your heart, too. When you laugh, your body releases nitric oxide, a powerful little molecule that helps your blood vessels open up, improves circulation, and reduces inflammation. In other words, laughing doesn't just lift your mood – it literally helps your heart beat happier and healthier.

So the next time you burst into laughter – snorting, crying, wheezing – know that something much deeper is happening. It's not just fun. It's a lifeline. A spark. A paddle in the water, heading back to connection.

Never – and I repeat, never – hold your laughter in just because you don't like the sound of it. And to hell with anyone who ever made you feel like your laugh wasn't enough. Whether you wheeze, snort, gasp, cackle, or do that silent shake followed by a loud bark – who cares? That sound is joy escaping your body, and it is perfect exactly as it is.

And to those members of society who have let out a sneaky fart while laughing hysterically – congratulations, because you've just reached peak human authenticity. What a gift you are to those around you, because chances are, if they heard it, they are laughing harder.

It's that moment when your laugh gets so real and your body decides to join the party. It's like your soul's way of saying, 'We are all in on this!'

Just own it, laugh louder, and remember – the best moments often come with an unexpected soundtrack. And sometimes, your laughter isn't just for you. I like to think the universe lines it up perfectly, sending it out like a ripple for someone who needs it – to lift their spirit, soften their day, or remind them they're not alone. A laugh can land like medicine, without us ever knowing.

When you hold your laughter in, all you're doing is depriving your system of the biochemical magic it needs to survive long-term. And worse, you're hiding a beautiful part of yourself in the process. You don't deserve that. So don't dim the sound of your joy for anyone, because you're also giving your heart a little tune-up while you're at it.

Make the sounds anyway. Let it rip. And as my late Aunty Izzy – who had the biggest, loudest laugh of all – used to say:

'Stick that in your pipe and smoke it!'

HA!

EMOTIONAL REGULATION THROUGH HUMOUR

Humour has an extraordinary way of cutting through tension. It doesn't erase the problem, but it can defuse the emotional bomb before it detonates. In moments of high stress, conflict, or disconnection, laughter acts like a pressure valve – releasing just enough steam to help us come back to ourselves and each other.

Here's an example for you.

I was once in a heated discussion with Dan – both of us frustrated, speaking sharply, eyebrows doing that thing. I can't even tell you what we were arguing about, but I remember that I was ready for my big finish. I was perched high on my soapbox, firing off points like a righteous debate champion, building to that glorious mic-drop moment. I imagined him left in stunned silence, thinking, 'She's right. What a wise woman I married.'

So, I launched into my final line – blah blah BLAH – and dramatically turned to leave the room. I marched off like my shit didn't stink … only for my dressing gown sleeve to catch on the door handle and slingshot me right back to where I started. What a humbling moment.

Dan paused, blinked, and then completely lost it. The snort-laugh started, followed by full-blown, can't-breathe, bent-over kind of laughter. Dan's laugh is gold, so naturally I had to purse my lips to not give in.

As far as I saw it, I had two options:

1. Unscrew the door handle and launch it across the room, or
2. Surrender to the ridiculousness – and give in to laughing with him.

Now yes, technically, he was laughing at me. But not in a mean-spirited way. It was the kind of laugh that says, 'This is too good, we both needed it – and I must have looked like a right tit.' I started laughing too – because what else can you do when your dramatic exit turns into slapstick comedy?

In that moment, everything softened. The argument dissolved. Our egos dropped away (mine, quite literally, was still hanging on the door handle). The emotional charge just … fizzled out.

That's the power of humour in emotional regulation.

It doesn't mean the problem vanishes, but it helps us reset. It brings perspective. It shifts us out of our reactive brain and back into connection – with ourselves, and with each other. And often, that's the very thing we need most.

Laughter is essential.

It's not just a nice little bonus when someone tells a good joke – it's a biological gift. Science backs it up: people who laugh regularly tend to live longer, healthier lives. But here's the thing – we forget to seek out joy. Why? Most of us are stuck in survival mode, bracing for the next disaster like it's lurking just around the corner.

Unless an actual bear is charging at you, it's probably safe to step out of fight-or-flight and unclench your jaw. We weren't built to live in fear 24/7. You're human first. We are wired to connect, and laughter – gorgeous, gut-shaking laughter – is still one of the best medicines we've got.

Indigenous communities around the world continue to show us this truth: laughter and connection aren't just 'nice-to-haves' – they're sacred. They are part of what keeps us well. Whole. Human.

THE OKINAWAN WAY: LONGEVITY, LAUGHTER & LIVING LIGHTLY

When we talk about wellness, it's easy to get swept up in trends – new supplements, gym routines, green powders, cold plunges. But sometimes, the most powerful wisdom comes from the people who've quietly been living well for over a century. And nowhere is that more evident than in Okinawa, Japan.

This little island, part of the Blue Zones – a term coined by Dan Buettner to describe regions with the highest concentrations of centenarians – holds an extraordinary secret. Its residents live longer, not because they chase health obsessively, but because they live in a way that's deeply joyful, connected, and balanced.

In Okinawa, there's a beautiful saying:

笑いは百薬の長

'Laughter is the best medicine'

And they mean it. Laughter is woven into their daily lives – shared between neighbours, during morning routines, in multigenerational homes, and over tea with friends. They don't just laugh when things are funny; they laugh because it's good for the spirit.

But it goes deeper than laughter. Okinawans practice something called 'ikigai' – your reason for being. It's not tied to status or productivity. It's about finding joy in the small things: growing vegetables, dancing in the kitchen, gossiping gently on the front porch, making miso soup for the grandkids, or walking with a neighbour at sunrise. Laughter and joy are daily nutrients – not weekend luxuries.

Kaizen, a Japanese principle, is all about small, consistent steps. Tiny changes, practiced regularly over time, can lead to big improvements. The same goes for happiness: learning to create little moments of joy, often and intentionally, helps it become second nature.

Even their social structures are built for longevity. Okinawans often belong to a 'moai,' a lifelong circle of friends who support each other emotionally, socially, and even financially if needed. These aren't surface-level connections – these are deep, decades-long relationships built on loyalty, laughter, and shared life. The kind of connection that lowers cortisol, raises oxytocin, and, yes, literally helps people live longer.

Now let's contrast that with the West. We've somehow convinced ourselves that isolation, burnout, and emotional suppression are markers of success. That if you're not hustling, grinding, and perfectly coping at all times, you're falling behind. We treat joy like dessert – something you earn after being 'good.'

But the Okinawan way reminds us of a profound truth: joy is part of health. Connection is part of healing. Laughter is medicine. And you don't need to wait for everything to be perfect to welcome it in.

In a book called *Ikigai – The Japanese Secret to a Long and Happy Life*, written by Hector Garcia and Francesc Miralles, Yuki, whom they interviewed, shares her secret to longevity: 'Smiling and having a good time.' She credits her energy and well-being to a rich social life and plenty of fun with friends.

One of the oldest women in the world, and in fact my hero, Umeto Yamashiro, lives in Okinawa, Japan. She says her secret to living to 103 – and counting – is simply to always have fun! Those are truly wise words. She also adds: 'I am in perfect health, have no illnesses, and take no medication. At my last medical exam, my doctor was jealous of my impeccable health. The secret? Laugh, laugh, laugh! Don't let anger, hatred, or worry take up space inside you. Be active, go out, party, dance, play music, and embrace life.'

These incredible Japanese centenarians live with fun and human connection at the heart of each day. They say keeping your heart young comes down to one simple truth: 'Spending time together and having fun is the only thing that matters.' Whether it's laughing, dancing, or playing games like gate-ball (think croquet with a Japanese twist), joy isn't just a bonus – it's essential. They don't just play, they savour it. They soak up every moment, feeling genuine gratitude for the experiences that light them up. For them, joy is non-negotiable – and honestly, that might just be the real secret to a long, happy life.

You don't reach 100, still sharp, walking, gardening, and playing games unless your mindset is about seeking joyful opportunities. Like Peter Attia reminds us, emotional suffering can seriously damage our health in every way. The part to remember? Happiness is a choice. If you're feeling lost and don't know your way out, this is how we learn to trigger it – through a style of play you'll truly love. No procrastinating, just pure joy. And once you discover what works for you, nothing can hold you back.

So, maybe your own version of 'ikigai' is dancing in your kitchen. Maybe it's calling a friend who always makes you laugh until your stomach hurts. Maybe it's watching ridiculous cat videos, walking in the park while talking absolute nonsense with your partner, or laughing at yourself when life throws you into a comedic face-plant – or door-knob shame in my case!

Because here's the thing: none of us are getting out of here alive –

but how we live until then? That's entirely up to us.

And if a woman who's lived more than a century says the secret is to laugh and have fun – well, I say we take her word for it.

The late and refreshingly progressive Pope Francis did something unexpected: he hosted more than 100 comedians from around the world at the Vatican. Big names like Whoopi Goldberg, Jimmy Fallon, Chris Rock, Stephen Colbert, and Conan O'Brien were invited to Rome, joining over 200 people from fifteen countries in a joyful, unconventional audience.

In a beautiful reminder of how vital laughter is, Pope Francis celebrated the importance of humour – even saying that laughing at God 'is not blasphemy.' Instead, he urged comedians to use their powerful gift to spread joy 'in the midst of so much gloomy news.'

'You unite people,' he said. 'Because laughter is contagious.'

He's absolutely right. Comedy has this rare, magical ability to cut through tension, bring people together, and remind us we're not alone. It's one of the few art forms where there's only one acceptable response: laughter. You don't walk out of a comedy show saying, 'Wow, that joke was really moving,' – you want to say, 'My face hurts from laughing.' If you barely laughed, it feels like something important was missing.

That's the beauty of it: humour connects us instantly. It bypasses the intellect, drops us into our bodies, and gives us a moment of shared relief, even in dark or heavy times.

Laughter has a way of making sadness feel smaller.

It lifts the weight from our shoulders with humour and ease. If we couldn't fix it – well, at least we could laugh about it – is something my family has always done.

My dear friend Kay Backhouse, who is a grief counsellor and author, says: 'The lines between joy and heartache can become blurred when we are grieving, and it can feel uncomfortable embracing both. But if we resist laughter and joy through feelings of guilt, we can create resistance and stagnation. Laughter is medicine. It's not a cliché, it's science. Laughing until we cry is like a mini baptism – cleansing, healing, a release. It feels good. It reminds me I am alive.'

HOW LAUGHTER HONOURS GRIEF

There's a misconception that grief must always be quiet and solemn. But laughter doesn't dishonour loss – it honours life. It's a way of saying, 'You mattered. You were loved. You brought us joy, and we're not letting that go.'

In that hospital room, we weren't laughing at death – we were laughing in defiance of it. Not to escape the pain, but to make room for something lighter to coexist alongside it. Because grief isn't one-dimensional. It's love, memory, longing – and sometimes, it's downright absurd. Like my Gran's to-do list before she left us: a vendetta against the neighbour's cat, making sure we got a refund on the new vacuum cleaner she'd bought the week before, and a deep fear of wasting the blueberries in the fridge. Bless my sweet Gran.

Laughter gave us a way to hold both joy and sorrow in the same breath. It reminded us that even in our darkest moments, we're still alive, still connected, still human.

So laugh. Even through your tears. Especially through your tears. It's not disrespectful – it's healing. It's sacred. And in many ways, it might just be the most honest tribute of all.

The only real enemy of laughter? Not finding a toilet in time. It's all fun and games until someone sneezes while giggling – or worse.

My mum is the funniest when this happens. She'll flip a table if she has to. She crosses her legs like a pretzel, grips the nearest ledge for dear life (even if that 'ledge' is one of us), and then charges like a footy player, hip-and-shouldering anyone who dares get between her and the nearest loo. At that point, it's less 'laugh until you cry' and more 'laugh and pray your pelvic floor's doing its job.'

So many women know this struggle. They'll launch across a room, hurdle a chair, or ditch a handbag mid-sprint if it means making it to the bathroom before the dam gives way. Sometimes they make it, sometimes they don't. Either way, they're still laughing – relieved in more ways than one, and usually one giggle away from needing a full outfit change.

Bless the light bladder-leak undies: the unsung heroes of laughter, trampolines, and surprise sneezes everywhere. MVPs of midlife, truly.

IF WE LAUGHED MORE, WHAT WOULD HAPPEN IN SOCIETY?

If society laughed more, we'd basically be healthier, happier, and way less likely to start arguments over pineapple on pizza. Laughter is like a free gym membership for your soul – it burns calories, boosts mood, and tightens those emotional abs. It helps us bond, makes awkward conversations less painful, and turns stressful moments into sitcom-worthy memories. If everyone cracked up more often, we might just crack fewer problems … and maybe even elect fewer clowns. Or at least funnier ones.

HOW DIFFERENT CULTURES MOURN

While many view mourning as strictly solemn, countless cultures around the world embrace laughter as a way to honour the dead and process grief. In Mexico's Día de los Muertos, families celebrate with jokes, music, and humorous poems for the departed. In New Orleans, jazz funerals blend sorrow with celebration – featuring lively parades, dancing, and brass bands that turn loss into a joyful send-off. At Irish and Scottish wakes, it is not unusual to encounter storytelling, laughter, and even a prank or two, offering a playful farewell to the dearly departed.

In Ghana and the Philippines, funerals can feel more like festivals, filled with funny stories and laughter meant to uplift the soul. The Toraja people in Indonesia even keep loved ones at home for weeks or months, continuing to talk, laugh, and live with them as part of the family. These rituals show us that laughter isn't disrespectful – it's reverent. It reminds us that love doesn't end with death, and joy doesn't have to stop at grief's door.

On my mum's side, we're Scottish; on my dad's side, Serbian. I know what you're thinking … what a fiery, wild combo.

One thing I've noticed is how differently the two cultures handle grief, especially when it comes to laughter.

My Deda (my dad's dad) wore black for a whole year after my Baka passed. He visited her grave every single day. No joy, no laughter – just sorrow. His heart was broken, understandably. But he also didn't allow himself to feel joy in her honour, because it felt like a betrayal.

And yet, my Baka was a vivacious, spirited, loud, full-of-personality woman. I have no doubt she'd have been yelling from the heavens, 'Miroslav! What are you doing?' She would have wanted him to laugh. To find lightness. To remember her in the funny and real moments they shared.

He had a stroke a few years later, coupled with a broken heart. But even now, I still wish I'd heard his cheeky laugh many more times before he went.

WHAT HAPPENS WHEN THE WALLS COME DOWN?

When we laugh, something beautiful happens: the walls come down. Laughter lowers our defences, encourages honesty, deepens relationships, and even sparks fresh thinking. It's like emotional WD-40, and suddenly everything moves a little more smoothly.

I co-host a podcast called *The Beautiful Nightmare* – the podcast for people who love good quality bullshit. We originally started out as *Motherhood: A Beautiful Nightmare*, but something didn't feel quite right. Over time, people began coming up to us saying, 'I listen to your podcast … but I'm not a mum – is that okay?' Or, 'I'm a bloke; is it weird that I listen and love it?'

That's when we realised the title was too limiting. It felt like a club that certain people weren't allowed into. And that didn't sit well with us, because no way is it weird – it's brilliant. So we dropped the 'motherhood' part and opened the doors wider. No club. Just laughs that anyone can listen to.

We won *Best Comedy Podcast* at the Australian Podcast Awards – an absolute honour and something Tamara and I will always treasure. But honestly, nothing means more to us than when our listeners take the time to message us. It's incredibly heartwarming when someone opens up and shares something vulnerable. One listener I'll never forget is a farmer's wife living in regional Queensland. She told us she loves her husband, her kids, and life on the land – but it can get lonely and isolating, especially as a young mum.

She said our podcast helped save her during the hardest parts of postnatal depression. We didn't know her personally, but somehow, through our laughs, honesty, and ridiculous banter, something reached her. It brought laughter into her life at a time she needed it most – and that, in turn, helped her begin to heal.

She didn't realise the magic she gave us just by sharing her story. I won't lie – I cried reading her message. It reminded me of why we do what we do, and it gave me hope that our podcast continues to reach the people who need a laugh ... even if they never tell us.

So, I hope I've sold you on the benefits of laughter – but like most ancient wisdom, this isn't news to you. It's the kind of knowing that already lives inside us. It just needs a little dusting off from time to time. Laughter, in and of itself, is life's tonic for almost anything. Not everything – but more than you might think.

CHAPTER SIX

CLOCK YOURSELF

'We have more time than we think'.
~ Laura Vanderkam ~

'It's worth pointing out – before I lose you to the classic 'I don't have time' excuse – that this isn't about cramming one more thing into your already busy schedule in the name of health and well-being. In fact, that triggers a stress response, and there is no need to do that.

CAULDRONS AND CHAOS

Throw back to our stressors as ingredients in our big, bubbling cauldrons – just toss 'em all in. The twit at the traffic lights, your teenager yelling for no reason, your partner chewing like it's a competitive sport, your sick parent, your wild toddler, the nosy neighbour, your hormones, your slave-driving boss… You get the picture. Then BOOM! One tiny thing tips you over the edge. You snap, all because of the proverbial cherry on top. And c'mon, who isn't shouting, 'There aren't enough hours in the day!'? Between 6,000 apps, an inbox full of school emails, and a corporate job that makes you feel like an underpaid robot, it's no wonder we're all running on fumes.

We are ridiculously time-poor and have limited mental bandwidth, failing to find time to live in the moment and have fun. If we can solve the time issue, does that mean we will feel less stressed and have more time for spontaneity?

CLOCKING YOUR LIFE (YES, REALLY)

I want to prove that you have more time in your day than you think. First, let's look at where you are allocating your time. It sounds a bit blunt, but we need to start taking ownership of what we do. Let's get serious here – record where you spend your time over a week:

- What happens from the moment you wake up until an hour has passed?
- What comes next?
- Making breakfast/lunches for the day?
- How long is your commute to work?
- What do you do during your lunch breaks? Do you take breaks?
- What happens after work?
- Do you spend time chatting on the phone? Is it productive, or is it drama-filled?
- What about texting?
- Scrolling?
- How much time do you spend procrastinating vs. productively working?
- Are you saying YES to too many things?
- Showering time? (I'm guilty here.)
- How much time do you spend watching TV or listening to podcasts?
- Housework?
- Tending to the needs of others, both physically and emotionally?
- What about exercise?
- How many times do you allow yourself to get distracted?

¤   Add your own here – these are just examples to get us started.

One minute, you're in the flow, and the next, your phone pings and suddenly you're elbow-deep in cat videos and conspiracy reels about what they really put in food. Or worse, you just pick it up for no reason, like some kind of muscle-memory magic trick, and five minutes later you're like, *Why am I holding this? What year is it?* I've done it so many times I've started apologising to myself. And don't even get me started on screen-time stats – those little pop-ups feel like a personal attack: *'You averaged 6 hours and 43 minutes today.'* Um, no I didn't. Lies. Some kind of digital slander. Sadly, it's just your brain getting high on knock-off dopamine. Again. Like a raccoon with a smartphone.

This can be a bit of a wake-up call, because noticing your habits and being honest about them is quite confronting. But it'll show you exactly where your priorities lie. Where is your energy going? Are you setting boundaries with the friends or family members who love to drag you into their drama? Use these questions as a checklist; no doubt you'll add more things to consider.

SWAPS, NOT SHAME

The point isn't to judge yourself – it's to get clear. When you see where your time and energy are actually going, you can start making swaps. And those swaps? That's where the magic happens – where you find space to bring back your fun.

American social psychologist and author Jonathan Haidt describes in his internationally best-selling book why we are such an anxious generation: *'We aren't allocating time to engage in playful activities that we enjoy.'* There is no denying that we have a list of responsibilities that cannot be compromised; however, if you clock yourself, you'll find windows of opportunity to take advantage of. Instead of organising dinner with friends, maybe choose a fun activity to all do instead. Every three months, I have dinner with a group of friends – because let's be real, without setting a date, we'd never actually catch up. This time, it was my turn to choose the place. But instead of the usual sit-down dinner, I had this wild urge to shake things up.

So, I said: forget the fork and knife – let's throw axes.

And let me tell you, it was one of the best nights we've ever had. We laughed until our faces hurt, blew off a ton of steam, picked up some unexpected new skills, and – bonus – we now know exactly who we'd want on our team if the world ever went sideways. Think zombie apocalypse …and your bestie is out front, hurling axes like a warrior princess on a mission to protect your life.

Turns out, nothing bonds a group quite like hurling sharp objects at a wall. Who knew? Our next outing was quad bike riding - it was so much fun. I'm so grateful to my friends who said yes to the weirdness without hesitation. I highly recommend these activities. They don't have to be group-only either - try them with your kids, spouse, or parents. Instead of a regular coffee date, create an opportunity for an experience.

WORKOUTS VS PLAYOUTS

I go to a kickboxing and HIIT gym that I love. The workouts are intense – it's serious business. But after one Saturday morning session, we decided to flip the script.

Thank you to Tash, the manager, who instantly said yes to what seemed like an absurd request. We'd secretly planned a water fight days earlier and came armed with water balloons and pistols.

Now, I won't lie – some people hesitated. My friend Katie didn't want to get her hair wet, and others said, *'I've got to rush home.'* Fair enough. But rather than push, I thought: what better way to invite someone into fun than to show them?

And guess what? It worked. One by one, those hesitant souls picked up water pistols, joined the chaos, and before long, everyone was soaked, laughing, and fully in fun mode. Katie was one of the last people standing. It was honestly beautiful to witness.

That moment highlighted something powerful: the difference between a workout and play. One is about meeting a goal and training with intention. The other? Free-flowing energy. Joy. Connection. And sometimes, that's exactly what we need most.

There are times to take things seriously – and times to seize for fun. This took only twenty-five minutes.

We can't have it all, all at once. Even your phone needs to recharge. So, what things can you swap out to enable you to have more fun? Your life isn't meant to be an escape room. Prioritise those moments of fun and look for ways to sneak them in. Energy flows where attention goes – Tony Robbins – in other words, if you want to find these moments, you will. Give energy to those things, and they expand.

EXCUSE-BUSTING 101

Excuses will pop up – you can count on it. But here's a simple trick: take a step back and play the observer. Pretend you're the third person in the conversation. Notice what excuses are bubbling up, write them down, then challenge each one with a counter-thought right next to it. You'll be surprised how quickly you can flip the script when you see it in black and white.

Example:

- ¤ Excuse: *'I don't have time.'*
- ¤ Opposing thought: *'I spend forty-five minutes scrolling at night – I could use that time to do something that actually fills my cup.'*

The point isn't to shame yourself. It's to call out your patterns gently and give yourself a chance to choose differently.

ROUTINE, FRIEND OR FOE?

The less routine, the more life. **Paulo Coelho**

I keep my head on straight by clinging to routine like it's a life raft – gym sessions, school drop-offs, and a dinner rotation so predictable my oven could cook it blindfolded. But lately, I've realised I'm so in check, it's borderline robotic. Routine and spontaneity are supposed to be a team – right now, spontaneity's been benched, and routine's doing victory laps.

Sometimes you can have too much of a good thing where routines are concerned.

You know how it goes – wake up, work, eat, sleep – repeat until you forget what day it is. It's easy to fall into autopilot, but if we're not careful, we become efficient machines with unmet human needs. Step out of the grind once in a while.

'Being content is a good thing, right?' some may say. Sure, but at the risk of unintentionally closing ourselves off to spontaneity and the bait that curiosity is throwing our way, being content is far too beige. I like the colour beige for interior design purposes – not for the way I live my life.

FLIP IT, SHAKE IT, SURPRISE IT

Purely for our amusement – yours and mine – pick one thing in your routine today and flip it on its head.

Walk to work, or take the weirdest route Google Maps has ever suggested. Leave your phone in your pocket at lunch and pretend it doesn't exist. Have breakfast for dinner, or better yet, eat dinner under the table with your family – just because you can.

Step into the shower fully clothed. Set up obstacles to jump over while doing the bath-and-bed routine. Prank call a friend – I've done this, and it's good for the soul. My father-in-law is still recovering from the last time I sent him into a mild tizzy.

Do something random, maybe even borderline stupid. I'm writing this from the bathtub with my laptop on the bath caddy, and let me tell you, it's thrilling and also stupid. The happy hormones don't lie – they'll light up your brain like it's throwing a fiesta. Break the routine. Shake up your day. Your nervous system will thank you with fireworks.

Stepping out of your comfort zone, even for just a few minutes, feels weird at first. That's when you know it's working, because your brain is learning something new. You're not here to serve your ego – you're here to get curious and surprised. Don't just play it safe. Jot down fun stuff to try in advance, because when you're in the mood for spontaneity, your brain will one hundred percent betray you, and you won't be able to think of things to do.

Permission to drop the balls you've been juggling and let them fall where they may – seize that moment and let off some steam. That damn routine will be waiting with bated breath for your return. Just be conscious to step out of it, because experiencing things is the whole reason we landed here in the first place, I'm sure of it.

CHAPTER SEVEN

CURIOSITY DID NOT KILL THE CAT

No great discovery was ever made without a bold guess.
~ Isaac Newton ~

Attention cat lovers, take this as a cue to breathe a sigh of relief, because your beloved ball of fluff is safe in the hands of curiosity – and so are you, for that matter.

If you're sitting there thinking, 'Okay, I'm in – but what's my thing? How do I trigger that happy feeling?' The answer? Curiosity. That's how you find your thing. Follow what sparks your interest, even just a little. It doesn't have to be big or groundbreaking – just enough to make you feel a tiny flicker of joy. That's your breadcrumb trail.

No drastic measures needed – seriously! Just notice what sparks your curiosity and tune into it. Your sense of fun lives wherever your curiosity wanders – the two are inextricably linked and is wildly undervalued for the power it holds.

PERMISSION TO WANDER

Forget the rules (spoiler: there aren't any). Curiosity helps us peek beyond the quiet limits we place on ourselves, with a mix of wonder and mischief.

Just imagine what you could uncover if you let your mind wander the way it naturally wants to – freely, playfully, and without permission.

As the old saying goes, curiosity is the heart of an open mind – and that's where all the good stuff begins.

One thing that I love discovering about people is what perks them up. What is it that is separate from their friends and families that pulls them in? We are all wired differently, and the things we are instinctively drawn towards aren't just accidental and random; it's like a match made in heaven – they seek us out, the same way that we find them.

Be a witness to your curiosity. Just say yes!

What's it trying to bait you with? Where's it subtly pulling your attention?

Oi, pssst. Look over there!

That little tug? That's energy wanting to move, and curiosity is where it all begins.

CUROSITY = BRAIN JUICE

As you've gathered by now, curiosity is more than just a trait – it's a powerful brain booster. Research shows that when we explore, learn, or follow our natural sense of wonder, our brains release dopamine. That little chemical hit makes us feel happier, more motivated, and mentally energised.

In other words, being curious isn't just good for your mind – it's biologically rewarding.

It's important to recognise that even the most brag-worthy healthy eating habits and gym routines won't fully support your well-being if your mind is constantly overwhelmed, overworked, or uninspired. True health is holistic. A curious, engaged mind helps balance the body's stress response, boosts emotional resilience, and reinforces the benefits of physical self-care.

So, don't underestimate the power of feeding your curiosity. Your brain and your body will thank you for it.

As we grow older, we're often taught to suppress our natural reactions, and in doing so, our inner sensitivity becomes dormant. But the closer we get to a childlike state of free self-expression, the better we begin to feel – more alive, more connected.

Poet and writer Dorothy Parker captured it beautifully when she said, 'The cure for boredom is curiosity. There is no cure for curiosity.'

Curiosity is guaranteed to open doors and spark new opportunities. So don't resist it – let it creep in. You'll start to notice subtle shifts and surprising changes.

And when they happen? That's when you earn your bragging rights. Wink.

Take a moment. Close your eyes and take a deep breath – in for two, hold for four, out for six. Then take eight normal, easy breaths. Relax. Allow yourself to sink into the present moment.

Now, picture yourself five years from now.

What do you notice about who you've become?

Are you content and grateful with your choices?

How do you approach your daily life?

Do you make yourself a priority?

Are you finding joy in small, meaningful moments?

Looking back at your past self and thinking, 'I wish I knew then what I know now'.

STOP, NOTICE, ACT!

Before we start, a quick warning: the moment your curiosity tugs at your attention, stop and notice it immediately. Within five seconds, your brain will kick in and start analysing, saying, 'Nah – too hard.' Don't give it the chance to shut you down. Trust that spark and how it makes you feel.

Here's the next step: a tiny, ten-second exercise. Give this a real shot – half-hearted attempts won't cut it. Dive in, see where it leads, and enjoy the ride.

Each day, make a note – on your phone or in a little notepad – of one thing that sparked your curiosity. Just one.

The key: do it in the moment it grabs your attention. Don't rely on your busy mind to remember it later before bed. You won't. So do it then and there.

That's how you begin to rewire your awareness – and make curiosity a daily habit.

It might start off like this – and that's perfectly normal:

- I'm curious why there are so many assholes on the roads lately.
- I'm curious why my kids don't listen.
- I'm curious why my husband chews his food so loudly – it's mashed potato, for fucks sake, why is he even chewing it?
- I'm curious why I don't have many friends.
- I'm curious why my teenager spends the entire weekend holed up in their room.
- I'm curious why female dragonflies fake their own death to avoid having sex with unwanted males?

(How good is that last one? A fact I heard – and I really hope it's true.)

My point is – you'll dribble for a bit. That's okay.

Then one day, you'll catch yourself saying something like:

'I saw this reel on Instagram today – it was a paddleboarder. I've always wanted to do that. I love being near water. I'm curious what that would be like.'

And just like that, your curiosity shifts – from frustration or observation to possibility. That's where the magic begins.

Examples:

I overheard a conversation today about a women's footy team for over fifties. When I was younger, that kind of thing just wasn't an option for girls.

I bumped into an old friend who told me he's into mountain biking in the hills – and he loves it. That sounds kind of epic.

I saw an ad for a new Netflix series about an incredible female chess player. I used to play chess when I was younger. I have no idea why I stopped. I think I'd like to pick it up again.

This morning, I went for a beach walk and saw a group of people doing cold dips. Apparently, the health benefits are amazing. I'm curious – how could I try that?

I heard a song with a wicked harmonica riff. Funny thing – I've always wanted to learn to play, just for fun. You know, casually start playing at a party and surprise everyone. I'm curious … how would I even start?

You get the idea.

The things that are baiting your attention will start to reveal themselves. The difference now? You're open. You're noticing what sparks your interest in the moment – and writing it down.

Your next step?
  Check it out.
  Follow the pull.
  Do some research.
  Read up.
  Make a call.
  Float the idea past a friend or partner (one who has your back and won't shut it down).
  Ask questions.

Stretch your awareness.

Expand your learning.

Because that's how curiosity stops being just a passing thought – and starts becoming momentum. You have the green light to explore new frontiers.

You're here, reading this, because something stirred your curiosity – and that's a beautiful place to begin.

LITTLE SPARKS, BIG MOMENTUM

So, you're feeling motivated. Curiosity's doing its job, and your mind's throwing all kinds of ideas at you – that's good!

But here's the thing: setting a goal isn't enough to make it stick. This is where your values come in. Take a little time to think about who you are now and what you'd like to shift, so you can grow into the best version of yourself.

When your goals align with what truly matters to you – like wanting to be more adventurous – they stop being one-off achievements and start becoming part of who you are. And that's where real, lasting change happens.

BOOMER DAD AND THE HARMONICA

My dad – bless him – always wanted to play the harmonica. What made him curious? I don't even think he knows. Maybe he saw it in a movie once and thought, 'That's brilliant.'

So he turns to Mum and says, 'I'm gonna try that!'

And in true boomer Dad fashion, he adds, 'Nah, don't need lessons. I'll just watch the free ones on that YouTube thingy.'

To his credit … he sat there and gave it a real go.

Mum's like, 'Go for it, love.'

In go the earplugs.

Cue Mum on the phone, pacing the hallway, trying to escape the room where Dad is tooting away – sounding like the harmonica itself was trying to tap out and call for help.

But here's the thing: he stuck with it.

He taught himself a little tune that he now plays when he's with his mates, drinking red wine and solving the world's problems – very boomer-esque, of course.

I was genuinely proud of my dad for giving something a go, following a random spark of curiosity, and having some honest-to-goodness fun with it. Deep down, although he'd probably say 'Yea-Nah' if I asked, I think he was subconsciously searching for something to add to his life just for enjoyment's sake.

I also think part of him wanted to impress my mum – proof that sometimes, curiosity and love make a surprisingly good team.

I have no doubt he followed his nose right to it – for him, it happened to be music. He can't sing and his dance moves are rigid, but he loves listening to music. So, I guess the harmonica it is.

TRUST YOURSELF

Allow your mind to tinker with curiosity. Trust how it makes you feel.

Curiosity isn't a skill you need to learn – it's not lost. It's just been sitting quietly in the wings, waiting for you to notice it and invite it in.

Curiosity creates opportunity.

Ask the question.

Listen for the answer.

Then ask the next question.

Once the curiosity is satisfied, the question fades – and a new one will take its place.

Curiosity rewards persistence. It thrives on determination.

Asking questions is key – but so is the willingness to act on what they uncover.

When you let curiosity in, things begin to shift, but it will test your commitment.

Life gets busy. Things get hard.

You can't find the time. A child is sick. Work is relentless. Obstacles pop up.

This is where determination and reminding yourself that even in the chaos, your curiosity – your desire to learn, grow, and explore – is worth making space for.

Life, as we know it, often pulls us away from our true nature, making it all too easy to drift into lives that feel hollow or directionless. We're constantly tempted by powerful incentives – money, power, attention, success – that can distract us from what truly matters.

That's not to say you can't enjoy success or wealth – we should – but don't let them define you. Set them aside for a moment and reconnect with who you really are. Let your curiosity and intuition work together as your internal compass. They're quieter than the noise of the world, but far more honest. Tune in and let them lead.

CHAPTER EIGHT

WHAT STANDS IN OUR WAY?

Most folks are as happy as they make up their minds to be.
~ Abraham Lincoln ~

By now, I hope we're all on the same page – your fun isn't just beneficial; it's a moral imperative. Finding something that sparks happiness and brings you alive isn't simply self-care – it's a responsibility you owe to yourself and to the people around you. Because when you're lit up, when you're doing something that brings you joy, you show up better in every part of your life.

Now comes the hardest part: getting started.

HIDING BEHIND SELF-DOUBT

The things we're good at are often hidden under our self-doubt.

When you truly start to believe it yourself, your outlook is very different. You have a glow about you that others may notice, and you can feel it. It's undeniable. One of the things I love most about us humans is that we are similar in many ways but so uniquely different.

In my early radio days, I hate to admit it, but I spent a lot of time trying to sound like someone else – someone, let's say, cooler than me. I'd listen to BBC Radio One and mimic the presenters: their tone, their flow, their so-called 'edge' – anything I thought I was missing.

It wasn't just my own insecurities driving this. A program director once told me, 'Sound like her – she's who you want to be.'

Oof. If that wasn't a clear message that I wasn't good enough as I was, I don't know what is.

All I heard in that moment was: Don't be you, Shanelle. And that stuck – and it hurt.

It took a long time to untangle that message. No matter how much love and praise I got from the people closest to me, it didn't feel like enough. Because they weren't the ones offering me the job. They weren't the gatekeepers. And when you're chasing a dream, it's easy to believe that fitting in is the only way forward – even if it means leaving parts of yourself behind.

I've always had a somewhat deep voice. Back in school, I was convinced I sounded like a prepubescent boy – and just in case I forgot, a couple of people were quick to remind me: 'Wow, your voice is deep for a girl, isn't it?' Yep, thanks for that. But funny how things turn out. That same voice is now one of my greatest assets and has ended up being my golden ticket. Would you believe that sounding like your own unique self is exactly the thing that makes you succeed?

RESISTANCE: FRIENDS, FAMILY AND THE HERD

Deciding – sometimes suddenly – that you want to inject more fun into your life can actually stir up a bit of resistance from those around you. Surprising, right? But people's beliefs (and our own long-held ones) have a sneaky way of shaping our thoughts and reactions. When you start stretching yourself in new ways, it can make others uncomfortable. Sometimes it holds up a mirror to their own insecurities.

Some people will cheer you on. Others might not – or simply won't know how. And that's okay. Some relationships may shift – and that's okay too. Because if you're being true to yourself, what more can you really ask for?

As you step in a new direction, seeking more joy and fun, you may notice some people around you are feeling challenged. You might unintentionally make them question the way they live – their routines, their choices, even their sense of what's 'right.' At first, their reactions may be defensive rather than thoughtful.

Don't get caught up in their resistance. If your choices have others questioning your sanity, you're likely on the right path. The way to know if it's right? Lead with your heart, not your ego.

'What the herd hates most is the one who thinks differently; it is not so much the opinion itself, but the audacity of wanting to think for themselves.' – Arthur Schopenhauer (1788–1860)

We need to detox our belief systems around this; it's too heavy for us to carry. Ancient wisdom holds many of the answers we're searching for in this lifetime, and the importance of fun is no exception. You have been given your life – think about how you want to respond to that. Facing the fact that we'll all die someday isn't something to fear, but a fuel to live fully.

MOTIVATION MATTERS (Even when it doesn't show up)

Think back: What did you love doing as a kid? Who was there with you? And as an adult, have you ever done something that made you feel alive laughing, screaming with excitement, totally caught up in the moment? And remember a feeling that isn't so foreign to you but may have been lying dormant.

Think about what motivates you. Go on, try. Do you feel stuck? Don't worry – you're not alone. Motivation is tricky, and we often get it wrong. Most of us assume it's something you either have or you don't.

But here's the truth, as psychologist Dr. Julie Smith says: 'Motivation is not a skill. Neither is it a fixed personality trait that we are either born with or without.'

Some days, you wake up ready to conquer the world. Other days

… even thinking about starting something new feels like too much. And that's okay. The key is having a starting point – because without it, motivation disappears faster than you can say, 'I'll do it tomorrow.'

FEAR, ANXIETY AND WHAT-IFS

So what actually gets in our way when we're trying to make changes and stop living on autopilot? Even when we've had a big wake-up call and feel fired up with motivation to do things differently … what sneaks in next? Anticipatory stress. AKA: the 'what ifs.' It's that lovely habit of worrying about things that haven't even happened yet. What if I fail? What if people judge me? What if I look ridiculous? We get ourselves into a complete tizzy over imaginary scenarios. And the wild part? We're talking about something as simple and joyful as playful fun – and still, we hesitate. We make excuses, stall, and forget that our own happiness matters. Why is that so hard to prioritise? Maybe it's time we stop asking, 'What if it goes wrong?' and start asking, 'What if it's exactly what we need?'

Are you feeling emotionally drained most of the time? Constantly tired? How often do you get sick? When was the last time you did something that truly nourished your soul – not just your schedule? And be honest: when was the last time you felt genuinely proud of yourself?

Do you find yourself pulling away, retreating at home, secretly hoping someone might notice and pull you back out? These are big, sensitive questions – and they can feel uncomfortable. But here's the truth: nothing good ever comes from staying stuck. I really believe life gives us small, powerful chances to show up for ourselves. If we stay still, nothing changes. But if we take even one step forward – just enough to peer through the trees – we start to see the magic waiting on the other side.

That magic? It's you, living the way you're meant to live.

TINY WINS

What we're really searching for are ways to trigger those happy feelings when we need them. Let's be real: no one feels happy all the time. That's not how it works. But the beauty of joy is that it stands out because we've known sadness, grief, or low moods. It's not about being in a constant state of bliss – it's about learning how to reconnect to joy when we need it most. You deserve to look back at yourself with admiration – for the choices you made, the steps you took, and how you showed up for yourself when it mattered most.

A fleeting thought may have been, 'Gosh, I've always wanted to try that ... but where do I even begin?' Some outlets – like mountain biking, playing an instrument, or learning a structured dance – do take a bit of skill and practice. That's where small goals come in. Benchmarks. Baby steps. And most importantly – patience! Because honestly, it's rare to nail something on the first go.

Think of a toddler learning to walk: they wobble, fall, cry, and get back up again. But once they take that first solid step – boom! Total elation. It's the same with us. Knowing we all have to start somewhere makes the process less intimidating.

BUMPS AND STUMBLES

Oh, there will be bumps. Like the time I tried to show my son how to do the worm – and ended up rolling my ankle so spectacularly you can only imagine what I looked like. Spoiler: I have no business teaching dance, but I charged in like J-Lo's long-lost cousin anyway. Then I spent the next hour hobbling around with an ice pack like it was a new fashion statement. After that disaster, I handed him my phone with a video tutorial and said, 'YouTube's got this one, mate,' and just like that, my dance career was over.

If the bumps mean you lose interest halfway through, that's just your dopamine waving a red flag – abort mission, no guilt. That lily pad was never the final destination, just a stepping stone showing you what doesn't spark joy. Now, leap on to the next one. Remember, this is supposed to be fun – that's the whole point. Even if you roll your ankle but enjoyed it, try it again once you've healed.

JOY ISN'T OPTIONAL

Trying new things can definitely trigger anxiety. If you haven't seen the children's movie *Inside Out 2* yet, I highly recommend it. I never fully understood anxiety until I saw it personified in a kids' film, playing out as an actual character.

There's one scene where the character Joy is trying to stop Anxiety from taking over the brain of young Riley. She says, 'I don't know how to stop Anxiety. Maybe we can't. Maybe this is what happens when you grow up … you feel less Joy.' That statement hit me in a way I didn't expect. It made me reflect – not just on myself, but on the people around me. And I desperately didn't want it to be true … but part of me thought that little blue-haired character might be onto something. We're not meant to feel less joy as we get older – we just start blocking it. We allow other emotions – like fear, stress, or self-doubt – to take over. But joy is still there. We just have to make space for it again.

We're not machines. Life brings pain, insecurity, and fear. And the tough truth? No one else can do the digging for us – we have to do that work ourselves.

Starting something new will feel uncomfortable and uncertain – and that's not just okay, it's essential. It means you're growing.

Sure, it's intimidating walking into a new place and instantly feeling on the back foot. I'm unfit. Uncoordinated. Not creative enough. Not strong enough. GAH – I'm just wasting everyone's time, including my own.

I felt exactly that walking into a kickboxing studio for the first time. I was totally out of my depth and seriously wished I had a wing woman with me. I tried to recruit a friend – any friend – but no one was keen. That's when it hit me: why was I depriving myself of something I was genuinely excited about, just because I couldn't find someone to come with me?

So I took the plunge. I stepped way out of my comfort zone. Put me in a room to talk to strangers? Totally fine. But ask me to find a partner in a room full of fit, confident strangers while I stand there thinking, *What if no one picks me?* – not so fine. Can you relate?

Here's the thing – I went. I got through the awkward newbie stage. And now? I've been going for ages, met great people, and I'm the first to welcome a newcomer.

If it helps, I'll put it this way: we are naturally hesitant when walking into somewhere new because our brain can't predict what will happen. It will automatically throw caution into the mix – it's actually doing its job.

But just because it can't predict the outcome doesn't mean we shouldn't move. In fact, that very unpredictability is proof that we may just be taking one of the best steps forward we've ever taken.

FEAR ISN'T REAL

It's worth reiterating that fear is an illusion, and it's your mind throwing you caution – *don't do that thing – you may make an ass of yourself.* My point is that those people who are already there and doing it well were once beginners feeling out of their depth. So learn, commit to the process, and see where you are in six months. No longer the newbie, I can guarantee it.

If your relationships – partner, kids, family, friends, or co-workers – are struggling, it sucks. But when they're good, nothing beats that feeling. Not everything will be perfect all the time, but the people who really get you can help you get through the tough stuff. For instance, your friends might save you when your teenager's driving you nuts (because let's be real, sometimes you just need a lifeline), or your spouse has your back if your co-worker is driving you up the wall. You get the idea.

We're not meant to go it alone. Even if you love your alone time (me too), we all need connections that recharge us. Not everyone's your vibe – and that's okay.

But the right people lift you up when you're stuck. I like to think of them as traffic lights. Some people put you straight into the red. Others slowly drain you to amber. And then there are the green lights – the ones who charge you right up.

These are the fun-seekers, the energy-boosters, the people you can be yourself with. You always leave each other in better shape than when you arrived.

DEPRESSION VS GRIEF

Depression and grief are not the same thing – the way it feels to me is that grief is love looking for somewhere to go. It's the pain of losing someone or something that mattered. Depression is the loss of feeling altogether, where even love and joy feel out of reach. You can't simply make grief disappear – but you can find tools to help carry it. If you're grieving and feel guilty even thinking about joy or fun, like it's some kind of betrayal, know this: you are not alone. Grief takes time, and so does healing. But just as your body needs rest, your heart needs moments of light, too. Think of your fun outlet as part of your self-care, right alongside sleep, good food, and movement. Moving your body can ease the emotional weight, giving you small, vital breaks from the heaviness. Grief is part of being human – we all face it in different ways and at different times. There's no right pace. But letting yourself feel joy again doesn't dishonour your loss. It honours your life.

Think of it as a therapeutic antidote to your grief, one that is a tool to help you move through the intense emotions, which otherwise can remain stagnant inside of you.

I won't tell anyone how to grieve – how can anyone? There's no one-size-fits-all for heartache. It's deeply personal.

But I do know this: when you gently trigger your happiness, you're reconnecting with a part of yourself that needs you, too.

So, if you're trying something new, don't beat yourself up if your first try at play doesn't go perfectly. A friend might cancel, the weather could suck, or you might roll your ankle attempting a fancy dance move. Assuming it'll always go wrong – or judging yourself harshly, like, 'I can't dance, I have no rhythm' – is just not true. A wise drag queen, Noxeema Jackson, once said, 'Check yourself, Loretta, before you wreck yourself.' And by 'check,' how are we talking to ourselves?

OUR OLD MIND MOVIE

Our brains lean on past information, so they often miss the bigger picture. That's why negativity feels so heavy. When we dwell on things and make them worse, our minds blow it out of proportion, kind of like using a highlighter with a double underline on the bad stuff. It's actually trying to protect us, hence the extra emphasis. But if you shift your focus, you can build new pathways to see things in a healthier, brighter light.

We're wired to chase what feels good – and here's the fun part: whatever you want is also pulling you closer. So, why this book? Probably because you're ready to shake things up and choose more fun.

Joy matters, especially now. Maybe you want to feel proud, let off some steam, or just stop being wound up like a spring. The quickest way? Grab your courage and keep it close. I like to imagine the Lion from *The Wizard of Oz* yelling, 'Courage!' at you – mane shaking, paws waving, the whole bit. Seriously, if you need a laugh, go Google his 'best bits.' Comedy gold.

What happens around us shows up inside us too. If someone snaps at you in the school car park, your body reacts – heart racing, stress chemicals flowing. It's not just in your head; your cells feel it too. Now imagine doing something you love – laughing, playing, having fun. Your body responds again, but this time with happy hormones.

This isn't just good vibes – it's real science. You can choose more of those feel-good moments by letting yourself play.

What emotions might be hiding in your subconscious, quietly holding you back? Your fun outlet is meant to free you – it's your reset button. It's where you get to explore, grow, and tap into who you really are. And spoiler alert: you're not finished yet. Not even close.

That old saying, 'you're all the person you'll ever be'? It's so limiting and unmotivating. You're still becoming.

The noise in your head might never fully go away, but you always get to choose how you respond to it. And chances are, if a friend or child came to you with the same worries, you'd meet them with compassion, not criticism. Offer yourself that same kindness – you deserve it just as much.

PERFECTION IS OVERRATED

And another one: 'Practice makes perfect'? Even schools have scrapped that idea. Perfection is an illusion – and frankly, it ruins the fun. Ditch it. Mistakes are how we learn.

I tell my kids, Summer and Ollie, that all the time. But it took me years to apply that same kindness to myself.

The very wise Brené Brown describes herself as 'a recovering perfectionist and an aspiring good-enoughist.' The moment I heard her say that, I thought, *Shit, that's me too!* I've learned the hard way more times than I'd like to admit, but these days I'm okay with getting it wrong.

It's like releasing a pressure valve. I'm not chasing perfect anymore – I'm giving myself the grace to grow instead.

Most of us, as adults, have a rocky relationship with failure. It often brings along self-doubt and sometimes even shame. But failure isn't who you are – it's simply part of how we learn, grow, and move forward.

BEING A PARENT

Parenthood deserves its own quiet space in this conversation – especially for women, who so often believe that putting themselves last is simply what they must do, that their own joy belongs at the very bottom of the list. We carry multitudes – we bend, stretch, break, heal, and basically become an emotional punching bag.

Our identities become tangled in the love we give our children and the weight of everyone else's expectations, until it's hard to even remember who we are beneath it all. And sadly, this self-sacrifice feels like the only path we know.

Empty nest syndrome sneaks up when we've been living life on our kids' schedules – the school runs, the Saturday sports, the late-night 'Mum/Dad, I need this tomorrow!' dash. Then suddenly, the house is quiet, and you're left thinking, 'Well … now what?' If we don't start finding joy for ourselves before they fly the coop, the silence can sting harder than stepping on a Lego in bare feet. So start now – pick up a hobby, book that trip, say yes to the things that make you feel alive. That way, when the kids are off chasing their adventures, you'll be chasing yours too (just with fewer laundry piles).

I say this as a mum – there's nothing noble about losing yourself. Putting yourself last doesn't make you stronger; it just brews quiet exhaustion and resentment.

Motherhood isn't meant to be a performance. We're not living in tribes anymore, yet we're still chasing impossible standards shaped by everyone else's expectations. It's time to question that.

I tell Summer and Ollie all the time, 'Mum doesn't have it all together.' This is my first time doing this, too – learning as I go, just like my parents did. None of us really know what we're doing; we're all figuring it out with love and hope.

And yes, putting your needs first feels almost impossible – unless you believe that caring for yourself *is* part of caring for them. Because it is.

It's no wonder so many of us – mums and dads alike – feel just one breath away from burning out. We glance at others who seem to have found that elusive balance and wonder what secret they're keeping. But really, we're all tangled in the same invisible script – a story handed down about how we should live, give, and hold it all together. Maybe the truest act of freedom is to recognise that story for what it is – and begin writing a softer, truer one of our own.

For me, that new story is rooted in something far bigger than myself. I am my own person, yes – but I am also deeply shaped by the love I have for my children. They stretch my heart in ways I never thought possible, keep my feet steady on the ground, and remind me every day of what really matters. They are my why, my anchor, and the purest teachers I've ever known when it comes to love without limits.

And on the days when the world feels too loud or heavy, it's that love that steadies me – helps me pause, breathe, and begin again, with a little more grace, honesty, and light.

Raising little ones is a beautiful chapter, but it isn't the whole story. Don't forget – so much of yours is still waiting to be written.

YOUR OWN STORY

Whether it's your partner, family, or friends, spending time apart is just as important as hanging out together. You're all fully-fledged humans with your own passions and quirks – not a package deal. Sharing space with respect, support, and love? That's where the magic happens. Let people be themselves – it's honestly the best gift you can give.

If you've been with your partner a while and the spark feels a bit dim, ask yourself: are they still your friend? Because friendship is the secret sauce. And if you feel like nurturing your current friendships or making new ones, do it – that's growth, not guilt.

Want to shake up a relationship rut? Find fun together. Make each other laugh. Start a mini prank war. Build moments that are good for both of you, not just one. It's one of the things I love most about Dan; he makes me laugh – a lot.

Ups and downs are part of the ride. The tough moments make the sweet ones even sweeter. But here's the thing – you can't pour from an empty cup. Take care of yourself, and suddenly everything else works a bit better.

We all need connection, and chances are, your partner is craving it too. So speak up – about feelings, hopes, and what lights you up. This is your joy journey, and figuring out what sparks it is part of the fun. Trust yourself, show up for yourself, and maybe, just maybe, the rest will fall into place.

CHAPTER NINE

BACK SEAT DRIVER

I am learning all the time. My tombstone will be my diploma.
~ Eartha Kitt ~

Thoughts are not facts. (Say it again: thoughts are not facts!)

They might be ideas, assumptions, mood-fuelled ramblings – or, let's be honest, full-blown delusions – but they're not cold, hard truths. And they're not always helpful.

There are plenty of 'influencers' behind our thoughts, not just the ones on Instagram. We're talking hormones, stress, lack of sleep, work drama, and even what we had for lunch. So of course, our thinking gets skewed. As Eckhart Tolle says, 'become the watcher of your thoughts. Let them pass like traffic, but don't let them take the wheel.' Because when we're running on empty, that inner critic loves to grab the mic like a backseat driver on a road trip you didn't sign up for.

CATASTROPHISING - FROM ZERO TO PANIC IN THREE SECONDS!

Catastrophising – ever heard of it? I bet you have. It's that unhelpful habit of jumping from zero to full-blown disaster in about three seconds flat. Suddenly, a simple curiosity about mountain climbing turns into, *'What if I fall and die? I have a family. I can't leave them! AHHHH!'*

Let's cool our jets for a sec.

Instead of leaping straight to the worst-case scenario, pause. Check your safety gear. Start with a smaller rock. Learn as you go. While your mind's racing like it's in the Indy 500, anxiety is quietly fuelling the drama. And it's tough to enjoy life when your brain's yelling 'DANGER!' every time you try something new. Try not to buy into the freak-out, the truth is, the suffering we create in our minds is usually far worse than reality.

Here's the kicker: once your brain gets spooked, it builds a full-blown PowerPoint presentation to back itself up – bullet points, animations, dramatic soundtrack and all – just to convince you that yes, you should stay emotionally barricaded forever.

FEAR LOVES DRAMA

Next thing you know, you're drained, frazzled, and yelling, *'Get me outta here!'* But here's the twist: running from fear only gives it more power. The trick? Stick around. Ask yourself what's really freaking you out. With practice (and fewer dramatic exits), your brain catches on: *'Oh … we're not dying? Cool.'* Fear shrinks, confidence grows. Boom. Progress.

One non-negotiable: you've got to do it yourself. If someone else does it for you, you risk relying on them to cope. This is your victory to win and trust me – it feels way better that way.

Think of it like this: if you bail when anxiety's peaking, your brain sets that level as the baseline for next time. But if you hang in there, let the wave pass, then move on – you teach your brain it's not nearly as scary as it thought. Small wins make a big difference. *'What doesn't kill you makes you stronger.'* Thank you, Kelly Clarkson.

THE BEST BRAIN TOOL - META-CONGNITION

Hands down, this is one of the best mind tools I've ever learned, and I have to share it. It's called meta-cognition and no, Facebook didn't invent it. Meta-cognition is about creating space between you and your thoughts. It helps you notice what's happening upstairs without being dragged into the drama. So, when your inner backseat driver pipes up with all your supposed flaws, don't engage – just observe. That's it. You are not your thoughts. You're the one watching them.

FIVE SECOND BRAIN HACK

Quick trick: if you feel like you're losing your shit – mentally unravelling, emotionally cooked, or just two seconds from snapping - try this. You know how little kids sob so hard they do that double inhale between cries? That hiccupy, shaky breath they take before calming down? Well, here's the thing: you don't have to be crying to do it. And it's genius.

Try it now. One deep inhale. Then a second quick little double sip of air at the top. And exhale.

This simple breath pattern is called a *physiological sigh* and it's one of your body's natural tools for calming down. When we're stressed or overwhelmed, our breathing gets shallow and tight, which keeps our nervous system on high alert. But this double inhale, followed by a long exhale, activates the parasympathetic nervous system – the part responsible for rest, recovery, and that sweet feeling of *'okay, I'm not in danger.'*

Scientifically, here's what's happening: the first inhale fills your lungs and starts oxygenating your body. The second, smaller inhale helps inflate the alveoli (tiny air sacs in the lungs) that may have collapsed slightly during shallow breathing. This improves carbon dioxide release when you exhale. And that long exhale? It signals to your brain and body that it's safe to relax. You're literally breathing yourself back to baseline.

It's a sign that tension is leaving the body – and often, you'll feel a wave of relief almost instantly. So, whether you're crying in the car, about to lose it mid-email, or just feeling stuck in your head, this tiny tool can create just enough space to shift your state.

It's free, takes five seconds, and your nervous system will thank you for it every time.

THOUGHTS ARE LIKE POPCORN (Messy, Noisy, Annoying)

The mind doesn't half know how to stir up chaos. It's like you've laid all your puzzle pieces out on the table, making sense of everything … then in barges your younger, slightly feral sibling and flips the whole thing just because you got the front seat on the family road trip. Thoughts are like that – messy, reactive, and often out for revenge over old emotional parking spots. Words can wound, but they can also heal. That's why elite athletes have coaches in their corner – to help reframe the noise and focus on the goal.

Your job as a human is to live as authentically as possible. You're supposed to mess up – that's part of the deal. But you're also meant to rise. When life tests you, take the hint. It's not trying to break you; it's asking, *'Do you want to grow from this?'* If the answer's yes, lean in. Push through. The good stuff lives on the other side.

I know when I'm feeling vulnerable, that inner critic loves to make a dramatic entrance. But spotting it is half the battle won.

THE YAPPY LITTLE PEST

Here's what I've found works: ask yourself – *who's in your car?* (Okay, I know that sounds odd, but stay with me.)

I'm in the driver's seat. Curiosity rides shotgun. And my inner critic? Yep, they're in the back seat. They have to come along – part of the crew, like it or not – but they don't get to touch the playlist or shout directions. Buckle them in and kindly tell them to shhh.

Your inner critic isn't the villain it pretends to be. It's more like a nervous eight-year-old with a megaphone. Totally lacking context, kind of annoying, but ultimately just trying to help in its own weird little way. Imagine a tiny chipmunk version, like Alvin (a bit chaotic) or Theodore (adorably anxious with glasses). Cute, yes. But still – back seat, please.

Take notice of what the little mooch is throwing at you. You might even want to write those thoughts down – not to show anyone (unless you feel safe enough to share them), but to see them for what they are: thoughts. Not facts. No validation, no worthiness – just noise. The little bugger will torment you if you let it.

Let's face it, they're coming from an eight-year-old fluff bum who'll say anything to get a reaction. Even if it's complete crap or so twisted out of context that the original moment it stemmed from is barely recognisable.

ADVICE FROM A LOVED ONE

What would you say to your best friend, or to your child (no matter their age), if they were struggling and needed a boost? You'd choose kind, honest, uplifting words – ones that reassure and remind them of their worth. Now say those same words to yourself. Not the harsh inner commentary that creeps in when you're feeling low, but the real encouragement you give to someone you love.

You deserve that same compassion, too.

Pay attention next time you're advising someone you care about – notice how it feels inside. Chances are, it feels lighter, more caring, more generous.

It's about building a new way of thinking. Because if we stop learning, what's left? You're not just changing your thoughts – you're learning a new language. One that speaks to yourself with kindness, truth, and care. And like any language, the more you practise, the more fluent you become.

Compassion belongs in the car, too. This passenger wants only the best for you. They know when you need a gentle hug, not a hook punch. They're there to remind you that you're having fun.

Sometimes these realisations hit hard – because deep down, you already knew them. But for whatever reason, you've been tuned out, closed off, asleep to what you truly need. And when the truth finally surfaces, it can sting or feel refreshing. You know it's something that would help you feel better ... so what gets in the way?

We often get so wrapped up in meeting everyone else's needs that we forget we have our own. Women tend to feel this deeply. But men aren't off the hook either; many have been conditioned to push their emotions aside, to be the strong one, the provider, the steady ship. And when those emotional needs stay buried, they don't disappear – they build.

Eventually, something small triggers a big reaction, and we're left thinking, *Where did that come from?* Reality is, it didn't come out of nowhere – it came from being human and needing care too.

I love the animated movies coming out these days. Sure, they're made for kids, but they're actually packed with powerful life lessons for adults, too. These films lay down solid emotional foundations, all beautifully wrapped in clever storylines, as mentioned earlier with *Inside Out 2*.

And the best part? Whether you're watching with your kids, grandkids, or just having a solo movie night, they remind us of things we already know deep down – truths we've just buried under the busyness of life. They strike a chord, spark a feeling, and for a fleeting moment, we remember.

The trick is not letting those moments slip away so quickly.

Highly recommend: *Elemental, Soul, Inside Out 1 & 2*, and *IF*. I'm not even embarrassed to admit I cried during nearly every one of them – not because they were sad, but because they spoke directly to my soul. I felt seen. Vulnerable. Human. And I know I'm not alone in that.

Out of all of them, *Soul* hit me the hardest. It's my favourite. But *IF* really stuck with me too. It reminded me that even as we grow older and become more independent, deep down we still crave care, connection, play, and freedom. That childlike wonder doesn't leave us; we just forget how to access it.

So, hats off to the filmmakers out there who are quietly weaving these big, important messages into stories for the next generation. Little do they know – or maybe they do – that we grown-ups are benefiting just as much. Because if we're still breathing, we get to choose differently. We get to change – and sometimes in an instant, if we want to.

When it comes to our inner backseat driver – the chipmunk of self-doubt – compassion goes a long way. The more we understand its fears and triggers, the lighter its grip on us becomes. That little voice is trying to keep us safe, but it only ever operates on surface-level alarms. It throws thoughts at us like popcorn, without giving us time to really explore where they're coming from.

Think of it like this: imagine a mum at the playground. Her child is determined to conquer the monkey bars. But she hesitates. 'They're too high, maybe try the swings instead?' she says, gently steering them away from the challenge. The child now has a choice: listen to her worry and play it safe or trust their instincts and go for it. If the child chooses courage and swings their way to the end, we all know what happens next: *'See, Mum, I knew I could do it!'* And Mum, half-terrified, half-beaming, watches her little one shine.

This same tug-of-war plays out inside us all the time. Our true self longs to try something new, to stretch, to grow. But our inner helicopter parent – our ego, our protective mind – wants to pull us back to safety, even if the threat is imaginary.

So next time that chipmunk starts flapping warning signals, smile, thank it for caring, and do the monkey bars anyway.

'Sticks and stones will break my bones, but words will never hurt me …' Yeah, right. And I suppose carbs don't count if you eat them standing up? Words hurt. A lot. Whether it's something cruel someone said ten years ago or the uninvited inner critic in your own head whispering sweet nothings like, *'You're a failure'*, the impact is real. Our minds love to keep us 'safe' by recycling old nonsense dressed up as truth. And because that voice sounds like us, we buy into it. For women, it might say, *'You have to hold everything together and never drop the ball.'* For men, it might sound like, *'Don't talk about your feelings – just carry on like an emotional IKEA shelf: wobbly, but holding it all up.'*

TRUTH BOMB

We all have messy bits. And as the wise Dr. Shefali says, we don't bemoan the rose for her thorns. So why shame ourselves for ours?

You are not your worst thoughts. You're the person still showing up – scratched, scattered, and trying. But remember this: broken crayons still colour.

We'll never be completely without fear – and honestly, we shouldn't be. Fear is what stops us from sticking our hand in boiling water or letting our kids run wild near a busy road. It has its place. But the key is learning how to tell the difference between helpful fear and the kind that just gets in the way. Don't fight fire with fire – or hate with hate. That just drains the energy you could be using to have some actual fun.

That's where the magic of meta-cognition comes in. When you create a little space between you and your inner chipmunk, you can start to see things more clearly. Ask yourself: *Is this fear genuinely keeping me safe, or is it just being dramatic again?* If it's the latter, kindly tell it to buckle up in the back seat. You're still driving.

YOU'RE HUMAN FIRST

'You're not a robot ... unless you are one' (I made someone laugh hard with that once). But seriously – my robot vacuum doesn't need joy or connection. You do. You're human, not a floor-sweeping appliance.

Sometimes making the happier choice can feel harder, but I promise, it's always better for you. Playful fun isn't supposed to be a challenge. You're not aiming for results (unless you're playing pickleball then, sure, go for gold). All it really asks is that you be present and enjoy yourself.

Living in the moment doesn't mean ignoring what's next. It just means giving your brain a break from constantly being in 'assessment mode.' Let the judgement sit this one out – fun doesn't need it.

You don't need approval from anyone outside yourself to fully own who you are. As another old saying goes, 'If you worry about what people think, you'll be owned by them.'

Also, don't let your own expectations drown you either. Your soul is here to experience life. And when we don't nourish that part of ourselves, we feel neglected and disconnected.

YOUR ATTENTION IS PRIME REAL ESTATE - CHOOSE WISELY!

One area we often forget we hold great power in is the choices we make – daily, hourly, moment to moment. We have more time on this planet than we realise, and it's never too late to choose differently.

If enough of us begin changing ourselves from the inside out, it will ripple and start to influence others. Because living in the past can give you a pretty distorted view of who you are now. And the real kicker? It quietly drains the energy you could be using for good stuff … like feeling lighter, doing things that bring you joy, or even cracking a smile for no reason at all.

That yappy little chipmunk in your head will throw anything at you to get your attention, including a rerun of that time things didn't go well. Suddenly, it's like, *'Nope! Not doing that again,'* and your brain hits play on a mental horror movie you didn't ask for.

Sometimes it even makes up drama out of thin air, just to keep you safely stuck in your comfort zone. Other times, it digs into old stuff – things people said to you as a kid, or outdated beliefs you picked up without even realising. *'Let's rehash that thing you did at age sixteen, shall we? WTF.'* Not fair.

It's like your chipmunk's got a projector, constantly flashing warnings on a big screen in your mind.

Remember – meta-cognition is your secret weapon.

It helps you step back and watch your thoughts like you're binge-watching a slightly chaotic reality show. Just observe. Be curious. It's fascinating when you realise how wild our minds can be.

It's a bit like that scene in *The Wizard of Oz* when Toto pulls back the curtain on the great and powerful Oz revealing an old man flapping about backstage, vulnerable and eventually crying through his ridiculously oversized moustache. It's all smoke and mirrors!

Now, when your adorable little chipmunk (aka your inner critic) starts yapping about in panic mode, thank it for its concern, gently buckle it into the back seat, give it a soft 'shhh', and slide into the front seat with your curiosity riding shotgun.

CHAPTER TEN

FRIENDSHIP

Be the friend you want to have.
~ Ralph Waldo Emerson ~

Be the friend you want to have. It's a quote that floats around in different forms, but I'm pretty sure we have Ralph Waldo Emerson to thank for the original. Either way, I love it – it's simple, and it hits.

It basically says: show up how you'd want someone to show up for you. If you want solid, ride-or-die friendships, be that kind of person first. And if you're into manifestation, this lines up with the whole *act-as-if* idea – when you act like you already have the kind of friendships you want, you naturally attract them.

I get the biggest grin on my face when my best pals send me reels of us in our senior years – living it up in Italy, zipping around on Vespas at seventy-five with an Aperol Spritz in hand. Helmet hair? Who cares. Bad knees? We'll strap them up and keep riding. Honestly, what a time to be alive.

But here's the thing: all this reel-and-meme sharing has deeper roots. It's planting a seed of what we can strive for fun-wise in our senior years. The trick is not to wait until then but start creating those laugh-out-loud, joy-filled moments in every chapter of your life.

FRIENDSHIP ON THE SCREEN (And Why It Matters)

We're seeing friendship getting the spotlight it deserves in TV shows like *Grace & Frankie, Sweet Magnolias, Dead to Me,* and movies like *First Wives Club, 9 to 5, Steel Magnolias, Bridesmaids, Bad Moms* ... the list goes on gloriously. And let's be clear – this isn't just about female friendships. The need for real, joy-filled connections runs deep, no matter your gender. Think *The Hangover* for blokes.

What all these shows and films highlight is the beauty of choosing joy with your people. Sure, there are ups and downs – friendship isn't all rosé and road trips – but the magic lies in those small, scattered moments of deep connection, shared laughs, and mutual mischief.

Grace & Frankie in particular, hit home for so many because it showed that no matter how old you are, it's never too late to find your people.

As Sandra Kring puts it, 'It's not the length of time we knew someone that makes them so special. It's what they brought into our lives.' You don't have to carry friendships from the schoolyard to make them count. Sometimes the most special ones are the people who showed up ... and never left. (Quote source: unknown.)

IT'S THE DIFFERENCES THAT MAKE IT WORK

The best friendships aren't built on sameness – they thrive on differences. Your quirks and theirs, the little 'are you serious right now?' moments – that's the good stuff. Those differences teach us patience, acceptance, and how to meet in the middle. And often, they're what give your friendship its real strength (and its funniest stories).

My friend Sammy and I are complete opposites – to the point of 'who even are you?' – but we share a deep connection and always agree on one thing: lying on the grass and looking up at the stars is therapy in just about every way imaginable.

Star sign comparisons are hilarious. Look up your traits and then compare them to your friend's. If he or she gives you the shits from time to time, I bet you'll laugh when you read some of the quirks that come with their star sign. For example, I'm a Pisces, and my friend Tanya is a Gemini. According to the laws of horoscopes, we shouldn't get along. But we absolutely do – and we thrive on roasting each other about our shortcomings any chance we get.

Life works similarly. The randomness of it all might look like chaos, but deep down, there's a quiet intelligence at play. The best part? We don't need to solve the mystery. We just need to lean into the joy of it, like saying yes to life's inside jokes.

And if someone looks at you sideways and says, 'What's got hold of you?' while you're embracing this way of living then that's your clue you're onto something. It means you're stepping outside the crowd, shaking off the pressure to conform, and leaning into what truly matters: joy, connection, and the freedom just to be you.

I HAVE ALL THE FRIENDS I NEED

I often hear people say things like, 'I've got all the friends I need,' or 'I barely have time to catch up with the friends I already have.' And while I get it – life is full, time is short – honestly, it makes me sad every time I hear it.

Why limit yourself when it comes to friendship? Connection is about the unexpected magic new people can bring into your life.

I truly believe – woo-woo or not – that the people who cross our paths are gifts. They often show up exactly when we need them, even if we don't realise it at the time. You never know what someone might bring into your life, or what you might offer them in return.

My friend Laura and I talk about this often. Sometimes it's the most random time and place when you meet someone, but if there's a spark – something pulling you together – go with it.

We're given these relationships for a reason. Your partner can't wear every village hat, and neither can your family. And if things get tough with your spouse, who do you turn to? That's where your friends – the family you choose – come in.

But friendships aren't automatic. We're not bound by joint bank accounts or bloodlines, so they can fade if we don't tend to them. They take time, intention, and effort. But when nurtured, they can carry you through some of life's hardest seasons.

FRIENDSHIPS TAKE WORK (But It's Worth It)

In many ways, a strong friendship is like a marriage – just without the mortgage or the matching towels.

We all need friends no matter how independent, introverted, or self-sufficient we think we are. Friendship isn't extra. It's essential for everyone.

Friendship doesn't always come in big, obvious packages. Sometimes it's the quiet connection with someone new that ends up unfolding into something unexpectedly meaningful. And maybe, just maybe, someone out there really needs your spark, your kindness, and your humour.

You could be the magic in someone else's day. And they might just be the magic in yours.

People change, grow, move away and, heartbreakingly, pass away. That's why I genuinely believe you can never have too many friends.

Mel Robbins puts it perfectly: to make a friendship work, you need three pillars; proximity, timing, and energy.

Are you in the same physical space? Are you in similar seasons of life? And is there that unmistakable spark when you're together?

Now, you don't need all three – some of the greatest loves of my life live interstate or overseas. But we still have the other two pillars holding strong. Some friendships have all three, and they thrive with beautiful ease. Others … well, sometimes there's one piece missing, and the connection falls away. And that's okay, too.

Not every friendship is meant to last forever, but everyone adds something valuable along the way.

PLATONIC HEARTBREAK HURTS TOO

I've had my heart broken more than once and it wasn't by a romantic partner. It was through friendship.

That kind of loss can ignite a deep grief, a quiet sorrow for what once was. Sometimes the energy between you shifts and no longer fits. Other times, someone gets hurt, and the repair just ... doesn't happen. Platonic heartbreak can hit just as hard – sometimes even harder – than a romantic one. And while we may throw on a brave face and keep moving, it still hurts.

Some friendships run their course and that's more than okay. But then there are the heartbreaks that come from losing a friend differently. They might move away. Life takes them in a new direction. Or maybe they gain their angel wings far too soon. Or they face an illness that forces you to imagine a life without them.

What I'm getting at is this: don't close yourself off to new friendships. Let them in. Let them surprise you. Because joy might come wrapped in the laughter of someone you haven't even met yet. And you? You might just be the medicine someone else needs to heal.

LONELINESS IS A MASSIVE ISSUE

According to Dacher Keltner in his book *Awe*, we now have one fewer close friend in our circles of care compared to just thirty years ago. That might not sound like much, but when it comes to emotional well-being, that one friend can make a huge difference.

Keltner also shares that forty percent of people report feeling lonely. That loneliness isn't just emotional – it has a biological impact too. He adds that the dorsal anterior cingulate cortex, the part of the brain that processes feelings of rejection and isolation, activates the body's inflammation response when we feel lonely. In other words, disconnection doesn't just hurt – it stresses the body.

Loneliness isn't just a passing feeling; it's becoming one of the biggest public health challenges of our time. Neuroscientist Dr. John Cacioppo, who spent years studying the effects of social isolation, found that chronic loneliness can raise your risk of dying early by up to twenty-six percent. That's no small number.

In today's industrialised world, about one in three people experience this kind of disconnection, with older adults being especially vulnerable. But as physician Dr. Gabor Maté points out, loneliness doesn't discriminate. It cuts across every lineage, income, background, and gender. No one is immune.

Even more surprising? Dr. Maté adds – loneliness spreads. Like a social virus, it moves through networks, quietly influencing the people around us. It's not just personal – it's collective. He adds, 'That's why it matters more than ever that we take it seriously.'

Spending time with your favourite people means more than just gathering around the table for food and drinks (though that's a bonus!). It's about actually doing something together – sharing an experience that brings you closer, like axe-throwing or quad biking. How random and also brilliant!

RIDE OR DIE

One of my all-time favourite movies is *The Wizard of Oz*. It's packed with unforgettable moments and some pretty powerful hidden messages. Take the scene where Dorothy feels worn out and ready to give up. But her three friends? They won't let her quit. We all need those kinds of people in our lives – those who lift us up and keep us moving forward, especially when things get dark. Whether friends or family, they're the ones who help us find our way back to the light.

There's real joy in finding a kind of fun outlet you can share – whether it's tossing a ball with your dog, dancing in the kitchen with your partner, or getting wildly competitive over board games with your friends (Monopoly may ruin relationships). This stuff doesn't just lift your mood – it opens the door to connection and is a powerful antidote to loneliness. It gets you out of your head and into real moments with real people. Plus, no one warns you about the incredible friends you'll meet later in life – the ones who feel like they've been part of your story all along. You'll catch yourself wondering, 'Where were you during my awkward haircut years?'

FINDING YOUR THING WITH YOUR PEOPLE

I MC for a number of Cheer & Dance events around the country. I'll sit there announcing for hours on end – from the tiny four-year-olds who'd rather play with the stage lights or pull things off their costumes (while their parents have spent a small fortune to get them there), right through to the elite athletes giving it everything they've got for a chance to compete at Worlds in Orlando, Florida – the mecca of cheer and dance.

But my absolute favourite routines? The adult novice divisions.

Why? Because watching them come alive and find such pure joy – when their main motivation is simply to have fun – nearly lifts me right out of my MC seat. I get a front-row view of their passion, their team spirit, and what it truly means to be part of something.

It's not easy to step out onto that floor when you're on the other side of forty or fifty, but here's what I know: choose your hard. That means choosing the hard you need to experience – because you will face one. The hard could be going out on the floor with your teammates and giving it your best, while battling nerves and your inner critic trying to hold you back. Or the other hard could be staying stuck, unmotivated, and possibly lonely, and not giving yourself that chance to find happiness. The same goes for an unhappy relationship – the hard of being a single parent, or the hard of staying in a relationship that makes you miserable. Choose your hard wisely.

I'm in awe of their courage to say yes to what lights them up –

to follow that inner nudge and throw themselves into the sport they love. Giving them a big, solid announcement to kick off their routine? It's the very least I can do. And watching them hug and unite after it is my favourite part.

COSMIC TIMING

At the end of the day, we're wired to connect – and laughing is still one of the best medicines around. The real difference between us isn't our abilities; it's what we enjoy doing. So, follow your curiosity – it has a funny way of leading you straight to your people. Be the kind of friend you'd love to have. Strike up the small talk, even if your nerves show up for it too. If you've ever wished someone would reach out to you when you're the new one, extend that same olive branch to someone else. You never know what might come of it. A kind word is like a spring day – Russian proverb.

And sure, sometimes you'll meet people who aren't quite your people – but they might unknowingly lead you one step closer to your own *Grace & Frankie*, or the male version – your Jack Lemmon and Walter Matthau (RIP).

You deserve people who love the real you. Not the polished version you bring to work, or the smile you put on at school pick-up, but the unfiltered you. The one with quirks, doubts, questionable jokes, and those clumsy 'figuring-life-out' moments.

The people who matter most aren't put off by any of it – they lean in. They don't just accept your flaws; they fold them into the reasons they love you. They're the ones who grab a seat in the front row of your life and cheer, no matter what kind of show you're putting on.

And here's the magic: those kinds of people make it easier to love yourself. Not because they deliver perfect pep talks or pen heartfelt birthday cards (though that's sweet), but because their unconditional love quietly proves something you might have forgotten – you don't need to be 'better' to be worthy. You already are.

Their acceptance becomes a mirror. One day, you catch a glimpse of yourself through their eyes, and for a moment, you see what they see: someone worthy, someone good, someone enough.

That's not weakness, by the way – that's healing. Because self-love isn't just an inside job; it's a relational one too. We grow in the context of connection. When someone else offers you kindness and consistency, it reminds your nervous system that you're safe ... and when you're safe, self-love has room to stretch out and settle in.

So yes, you deserve love. But not just any love. You deserve the kind that makes you braver, softer, more yourself. And you deserve to give that back, too.

Be yourself, because the right people will find you – and real friendships will rise to meet you.

IT'S A TWO PLAYER GAME

If you feel like you're always the one putting in the effort without receiving the same care in return, you're not alone. Many of us reach a point where we notice the balance is off. That's a signal to pause and ask: What are my expectations? Are they fair? And do I need to seek out people who are more aligned with my frequency right now?

Friendships shift with seasons. Some fade, some deepen, and others appear when you least expect them. The important thing is trusting yourself to recognise who truly adds to your life and giving your time and energy to those connections.

Also, just back on those friends that you meet in your midlife era – the ones who land in your world and make you wonder how you ever did life without them. It's almost eerie ... like, did they just materialise the moment you needed them most? Or were you both orbiting each other for years, waiting for the right timing to collide? Either way, it's magic. Thank you, Universe – what an absolute gift.

These friendships aren't built on shared classes or schoolyard games like the old days. They're forged in the fire of real life – through raw conversations, belly laughs, honest advice, and showing up even when things are messy. These are the friends who remind you who you are, who mirror back your best parts (even when you forget they exist), and who cheer you on in the most unfiltered, no-nonsense kind of way.

They're proof that soulmates come in all forms and sometimes, they show up just when you thought you had enough friends or were too tired to make new ones. But there they are, sliding into your life like they'd always belonged.

When it comes to really getting to know someone, conversation will only take you so far. It's in the unscripted, light-hearted moments – the ones where people forget to filter – that the real stuff shows up. That's why I love this quote from Plato:

'You can discover more about a person in an hour of play than in a year of conversation.'

It's a reminder that fun times can reveal a person's character in ways small talk never can. Whether someone's competitive, generous, curious, awkward, or wildly creative – it brings it all to the surface. It's a connection without the performance.

CHAPTER ELEVEN

EMOTIONS ARE THEIR OWN WILD BEASTS

There is only one way to learn - and it's through action.
~ Paul Coelho, The Alchemist ~

Emotional health isn't just mental health's sidekick; it's its own wild beast. While your brain's busy trying to solve problems like a detective, your emotions are the messy crew throwing curveballs. Your emotional and physical health have to tag-team, or else your vulnerabilities throw a tantrum. Put it this way: your body can be in tip-top shape, but emotionally, you can still be a hot mess. You can be crushing kale salads and smashing spin classes, but if you're emotionally wiped out and out of touch with yourself, none of it matters.

Emotional health deserves its own spotlight, not just tossed into the 'mental health' mix like it's the laundry. Play's the emotional circuit breaker which flips the switch when your feelings start short-circuiting and saves you from total rumination overload. Consider these questions: How stuck are you in your thinking? How often do you surprise yourself? And most importantly, do you know what lights you up? If not, it's time to find out.

According to research, happiness hits a low around just over age forty-seven. Not a midlife crisis exactly, more like a midlife meh. You're not losing it, you're not alone, and you're not broken. Here's what might be going on:

THE USUAL SUSPECTS

Career Stagnation
You've been at it for years, and now ... It's just emails, meetings, and the occasional existential dread. Promotions slow down, passion dims, and you start Googling, 'How to open a bookstore in Tuscany.'

Family Chaos
You're the human equivalent of duct tape – holding together kids, aging parents, and possibly a partner also having a crisis. It's exhausting, and you can't even nap without someone calling your name. Also, relationship pressures are a big one.

Money Stress
Retirement is creeping closer, bills are constant, and somehow your bank account didn't get the memo. Suddenly, buying that fancy blender feels like a reckless life decision.

Health Surprises
Your body starts giving you random aches as a hobby. You tweak your back sleeping wrong and need two days to recover from dancing at a wedding.

Unmet Dreams
This is when the 'Wasn't I supposed to live in Paris for a year/start a business/become a chef?' questions hit. It's a weird, wistful feeling that's totally normal.

The Good News? This slump doesn't last forever. Many people report being happier after midlife. You've still got time, energy, and probably better taste in wine. So take a breath, find your joy, and maybe hold off on buying that hot set of wheels ... unless it really sparks joy.

If this stuff goes unchecked, your stressors and constant rumination can quietly spiral into something much darker – burnout, substance use, or even thoughts like, 'What's the point?' But here's the thing: everything in life is fixable, and I mean that with complete sincerity.

EMOTIONAL WI-FI (Check Your Signal)

The real danger usually isn't one dramatic event: it's the slow roll into misery. Emotional health is like your internal Wi-Fi: if it's not working, nothing else really functions properly either. Yet so many of us ignore the red flags – stress, irritability, total exhaustion – because honestly, who has time to 'feel their feelings' between deadlines, dinner prep, and the never-ending group chat?

And let's be real: sometimes we don't even know how to feel them. Or we don't recognise that we need to. Big 'T' trauma or little 't' trauma, it all counts, and it all deserves attention.

Emotional health matters – hugely. It's how we manage stress, set boundaries, ask for what we need (without yelling), and stop numbing ourselves with habits that hurt more than help. It's not about being 'fixed' or perfectly zen – it's about learning to ride the waves without drowning in them.

You can't always change your circumstances, but you can change your coping habits. And that shift? It can literally change your mood. Think of it as self-management with soul. You don't need to have it all figured out.

MOTIVATION COMES AND IT GOES

It's hard to motivate yourself (or anyone else) when you're in a dark place. Everything feels like too much – the dishes, the texts, the 'what's the point?' thoughts. But – life is the point. And while you can't change someone else's behaviour, you can model something different. You can start small. And of course, you should start small with yourself, too. Rome wasn't built in a day, and neither is emotional resilience.

We can't be put in a box. There's no one-size-fits-all solution. We're messy, complex, beautiful beings – imperfect, wounded, vulnerable, and trying to make sense of life as we go. If someone around you is struggling emotionally, tell them they matter. Show them. Invite them into small, joyful moments, watch silly videos, go for a walk, laugh at panda fails. Start light and small. Because miracles don't happen overnight, but little sparks of joy, repeated often, can start to shift everything.

And if you're the one struggling, please know: you are not your thoughts. It might feel impossible right now, but the truth is, the only person who can fully pull you out and believe in you … is you. No partner, parent, or friend can do it for you. They can cheer you on, but you are the one who matters most here; you have to have your own back.

Be a friend to yourself first, before you try to be one to anyone else.

RAW TRUTH

Suicide is heartbreakingly common. So many people are suffering silently, smiling through pain, hiding their struggles, and seeming like they're coping. When they're gone, those left behind are left wondering what signs they missed and how they could've helped.

There is always another way. Someone will listen. Someone wants to help. If it's not your family, it might be your friends, or maybe even friends you haven't met yet, waiting on the other side of one brave step forward.

We can't erase our trauma, but we can soften it with our chosen fun outlet. One bout of fun won't fix everything, but a hundred little joyful moments can begin to shift your emotional world. Start there. Start small. And please, don't stop. Remember, if we just used laughter for the good stuff, we miss out on one of humour's greatest gifts. We need it to survive the hard times too, maybe even more so.

Imagine if you could just say, 'Hey Siri, set me to happy and relaxed today, and crank up the self-worth while you're at it.' Instead, emotions crash in and out like waves on a beach, doing their own thing whenever they please.

Just a twenty-minute walk in nature – without checking your phone – can totally melt stress away. The secret? Ignoring your phone. Because science says even if it's just chilling nearby, your brain gets all jittery like, 'Wait, did I miss a text? Or am I needed for something?'

Your brain's doing its best with what it's got – piecing together whatever clues it can to figure out what's going on. The result? Emotions. Loud and totally convincing ... but not always accurate.

ENERGY (The Good And The Bad)

Our bodies are more than just flesh and bones – they're alive with pulsing energy. And emotions? They're not simply feelings; they're waves of vibration, energy flowing through us in constant motion. Author Don Tolman puts it like this: 'Emotion is energy movement – it's our thoughts that create our emotions, and our emotions that create our behaviours.'

When we hold onto unprocessed emotions, old wounds, and buried traumas, they don't just disappear – they sit in our nervous system like static, waiting to be released. As the old saying goes, 'The body doesn't forget what the mind tries to ignore.' When we don't let ourselves fully feel an emotion, it doesn't just vanish – it digs in and settles somewhere inside us. If you don't process it, your body files it away ... usually in the least convenient place.

Because if you don't feel it, you store it.

Forrest Monk and author Björn Natthiko Lindeblad once said, 'Our thoughts are our conditioned thinking patterns.'

Most of the voices in our head, the ones that criticise, doubt, or second-guess aren't really ours. They're echoes of things we picked up early in life: someone else's judgement, society's expectations, old fears dressed up as facts.

THE REMEDY

But here's the good news: if those thoughts were absorbed, not born, they don't deserve all that power. You can meet them with the same indifference you give to random background noise, because that's all they are.

Get curious with yourself – not critical. Start by asking:

- Why don't I make finding fun a priority?
- Is it because I've been wired to equate productivity with worth? Or maybe joy feels indulgent, like something I have to earn rather than something I deserve?
- What stands in my way of finding a form of play?
- Is it time? Guilt? Fear of looking silly? Maybe I've just forgotten what lights me up because I've been in survival mode for so long.
- What thoughts or triggers come up when I want to explore something fun but can't seem to move?
- Am I telling myself it's not 'useful' enough? Do I feel like I don't have permission to enjoy something just for the sake of it?

Curiosity opens the door gently. No pressure, no judgement, just questions that lead you back to yourself.

We're not chasing perfection here – not even close. In fact, perfection's such a dirty word, I can't stand it!

Emotions come and go, but they hit hardest when we're running on empty. Our cauldrons aren't gently simmering – they're bubbling over. That's when everything feels too much, and the smallest thing can send us into a flood of tears or a full-blown adult tantrum. A remedy? See below.

EMOTIONAL FIRST AID KIT

Most of us have a first aid kit at home for cuts, stings, bumps, and mystery bruises we can't explain. But here's the real question: do you have an emotional first aid kit? No word of a lie – having one can seriously boost your stress resilience.

Those sucker punches to your self-worth or the sting to your confidence hurt just as much (if not more) than banging your funny bone on the corner of a table. Yet we'll slap a band-aid on a paper cut but bury emotional wounds like they're last year's tax receipts. Why? Because physical pain comes with instructions … and emotions come with awkward avoidance.

The good news? Emotions can be treated – just not with gauze and antiseptic. So, let's build your emotional first aid kit.

When your emotional first aid kit needs to come out, don't just grab a tissue. Move your body. Do something that pulls your brain out of the spiral.

Your brain can only focus on one thing at a time - either stuck ruminating or fully engaged. That's why having your kit ready before you need it is key. Build it when you're feeling proactive, so when the low hits, you're not starting from zero.

When the mood dips or anxiety creeps in, it can feel impossible to pull yourself up. However, if your kit is ready, all you need to do is open it, glance at your notes, and begin your chosen move.

One small step - sidestep the spiral and grab your kit - and suddenly, relief starts flowing.

Here are some ideas for your emotional first aid kit – because sometimes, the best way to reset your brain is to do something that shifts the energy:

- ¤ Move your body – in any way you can. Tap, shake it out, walk, work out … whatever works
- ¤ Fidget toys – stress balls, spinners, anything you can squeeze or spin
- ¤ Sports – golf, paddleboarding, boxing, tai chi, skipping, trampoline, tennis … movement is so good!
- ¤ Crossword puzzles or chess – for when your brain needs a focused challenge instead of a spiral

- Walk in nature – no Wi-Fi, no doomscrolling
- Blast a banging playlist – dance, headbang, lip-sync like it's a one-person concert
- Card games or a catch-up with a friend – adult playdates are so underrated for the power they have to shift a mood
- A task that gets you moving and makes you feel good – bonus points if it also makes you laugh
- Cooking for fun – no pressure, no fancy plating, just food and flow
- Make a decision – anything! Choose a new podcast or book
- Paint or draw – bad art encouraged; you don't need to be good at it
- Change your scenery – go outside, switch rooms, sit somewhere new. Shift space, shift headspace
- Tackle a small task – fix one annoying thing

Add anything that your curiosity has pulled you to prior!

Warning: No Social Media. Yes, you think you're going on to watch inspirational videos to boost your mood, but the algorithm has other ideas. One second it's positive affirmations, the next it's a video that hits too close to home, and suddenly you're spiralling. Best to give your brain a break from the scroll. Mute the noise, your mind will thank you.

I remember a time I was an inch away from meltdown city, no one was listening, the house was a tip, and my brain felt fried. The cauldron was at full boil. Then I spotted the kids' trampoline on the lawn. I said nothing, marched outside, and started jumping. Up, down, up, down, feeling the flow and watching that stagnant, negative energy slowly melt away.

Then Summer and Ollie spotted me mid-air. They gasped and yelled, 'MUM ... YAY!' They shot outside ... but their feet went nowhere. Dan had grabbed their jumper hoods and said, 'Hold it right there – leave Mum, she just needs a minute.' They agreed ... sort of, hopping in place, banging on the glass, and waving like tiny cheer squads.

The point? I jumped. I moved. And suddenly my mood lifted like magic. The annoyances were still there, sure, but I could handle them because I'd taken the edge off, no longer a pressure cooker ready to explode. Trampoline therapy: ten out of ten, highly recommend.

TAPPING OUT

Break the cycle and reboot your mood. I call it 'Tapping Out' (because I love martial arts).

If I'm feeling low, the last thing I need is to double down on the heavy stuff – like watching a dark movie, reading a book that digs into trauma, or spending time with those red or amber light people. That's my cue: Tap Out. I'll throw on a funny podcast, crank the music that lifts me, move my body – whatever shifts the energy. It's a reset button. Simple, but powerful. Remember – it's your cue to Tap Out.

And if you're lucky enough to have people in your corner – someone who feels safe, grounded, and solid (like a good friend or partner) – use them. Text or call and simply say:

'I'm running on empty, boo. I need to Tap Out.'

No need for a long explanation. The right people will get it, and they'll show up. Also, if you're still searching for your people, that's okay too. Start by following your curiosity; sign up for that class, join the group, try the thing that's been tugging at your interest. Chances are, your people are already there, just waiting for you to show up too.

Consistency is key because low moods don't care about your

schedule. Sometimes they come swinging with a roundhouse kick straight to your confidence. The trick isn't avoiding the hits – it's choosing not to beat yourself up when they land. Tap Out.

Every time you reach for your emotional first aid kit – whether it's texting a friend, blasting your favourite song, or diving into something fun – you're doing something powerful. You're training your brain, rewiring it with healthier habits, and slowly replacing the old ones that kept you stuck in the emotional ring, taking hits with no defence.

You're not just surviving the fight – you're learning to throw better punches.

GENERATIONAL COMPARISON

As Theodore Roosevelt wisely said, 'Comparison is the thief of joy.' Instead of letting yourself feel like you come up short when you see what others are doing, use it as a little kick up the bum. Let it motivate you to make your own move. Don't compare – just take note, then keep your eyes on your own path and keep moving forward.

One thing we really shouldn't compare is the following:

Baby Boomers (1946–1964), Generation X (1965–1979), Millennials (1981–1995), Generation Z (1995–2014), Generation Alpha (2015–2030).

We really shouldn't compare generations, unless it's a dance-off, in which case, Gen X will bring the grunge, Millennials will fist pump, and Gen Z will somehow make it look like a TikTok tutorial gone viral.

But seriously, here's why generation comparisons don't help anyone:

1. **Totally Different User Manuals**
   Boomers grew up with rotary phones and encyclopedias. Gen Z has AI in their pocket and grew up asking Siri the meaning of life. Different tools = different lives.

Comparing is like judging a fish for not knowing how to ride a bike.

2. **It Oversimplifies the Chaos**
   Labelling Gen Z as 'too sensitive' or Millennials as 'entitled' is like describing a flaming rollercoaster with 'it's kinda warm.' Every generation is dealing with its own dumpster fire, just in a slightly different format.

3. **Shifting Definitions of Success**
   Boomers saved for a house. Millennials saved for brunch. Gen Z is saving the planet. Everyone's winning in their own weird way.

4. **Blame Gets You Nowhere**
   When we compare, we often point fingers – 'They're lazy,' 'They're out of touch,' 'They ruined the economy!' Spoiler: it was probably more complicated than that.

5. **Each Generation Has Its Superpower**
   Boomers have grit. Gen X has chill. Millennials have memes. Gen Z has zero tolerance for BS and emotional burnout. Imagine what we could do if we teamed up instead of rolling our eyes at each other.

As a Millennial, I think it's worth pointing out that we dodged a bit of a digital bullet. Social media didn't become a daily habit for us until we were mostly through puberty – a time when our brains were already doing somersaults without the added pressure of filters, likes, and perfectly curated lives.

Gen Z, on the other hand, has been deep in the scroll since their formative years. Puberty alone is like living in an emotional theme park – throw in 24/7 exposure to curated perfection, constant comparison, and the algorithm whispering in your ear, and it's no wonder this generation is facing a unique mental health landscape. It's very worrying.

The big question is: what are young people being exposed to during those critical years of brain development? Because it's not just dance challenges and dog videos – it's beauty standards, success pressure, fear-based news cycles, and relentless self-comparison. That stuff sticks when your identity is still under construction.

If you're Gen Z and reading this, I say this with care, not criticism: the fact that social media has been part of your life while your brain was still wiring itself is a big deal. Puberty is already chaotic, and adding the constant stream of comparison, unrealistic standards, and pressure to perform? That's a lot for any developing mind to carry.

It's not about blame – it's about awareness. The more you understand what your brain has been up against, the more power you have to protect your mental health, set boundaries, and create space for the real, offline joy that every generation, no matter the era – truly needs.

So rather than compare generations like it's some weird Olympics of 'Who Had It Worse,' let's just agree on this: if you're alive in this era, congrats – you've made it through dial-up internet, Y2K panic, COVID, and at least one social media identity crisis. That deserves a medal in itself.

But here's one universal truth that hasn't changed across any generation: the need for fun and the ability to spark joy on purpose. It doesn't matter if you grew up with cassette tapes or TikTok – your brain still lights up the same way when you laugh, dance, build something, or lose track of time doing something fun.

So whatever your age or era, don't forget to hit pause on the serious stuff and do something just because it feels good.

WHEN IT HITS DIFFERENT

Some days just hit differently, though. You wake up feeling off – flat, fragile, like your brain's decided to turn the volume up on every minor irritation and sad thought. Suddenly, even your to-do list feels like a doom prophecy.

Ask yourself what's wrong, and you'd probably shrug. It's never just one thing – it's a hundred tiny things bubbling in our cauldrons, plotting against us. That's your cue: Tap Out and throw in something fun before your brain files a full-blown complaint.

Life isn't slowing down: hormones, deadlines, existential dread … it's a non-stop circus. And ladies, throw in periods, perimenopause, or full-blown menopause, and suddenly we're paddling upstream in a soggy paper canoe while juggling flaming torches.

When you're low, your brain goes into 'problem-solving mode.' It starts pulling files from your emotional archives, most of which are unhelpfully dramatic: You're not doing enough. How about our regrets? Remember that thing from 2009? The brain is a bit of a troll sometimes. It also tends to seek out evidence to match your mood, which is why everything feels like a sad song with no skip button.

But here's where play comes in – not as a fix-all, but as a relief valve. It doesn't erase your stress, but it gives your system a breather.

You don't need to feel joyful to seek out fun – you do it to find your way back to joy.

The sad part is that not only do we often avoid prioritising it, we stay stuck, ignoring that quiet inner nudge to shift our current situation.

If you're anything like me, you probably feel most 'in control' when you bottle everything up, tell no one, and wait for the emotional storm to pass. Spoiler alert: it's not healthy. It's one thing I've changed, and I've truly felt the rewards – namely, some inner peace and a more relaxed attitude.

So many of us suffer in silence, carrying on like everything's fine because we don't want to burden the people we love. There's also that sneaky little myth floating around – that if we talk about our problems, we'll just make them worse. But let's flip that on its head.

Talking it out with someone who truly has your back – whether it's a friend, partner, or family member – can actually shrink the problem. A hug, a bit of emotional backup, a fresh perspective, even just being heard without judgement … it all helps.

Any time I finally admit to someone close that I've had a rough week, the first thing they ask is: 'Why didn't you say something sooner?'

And honestly? Fair question. What am I doing sitting in my own head like a moody hermit when I have people who want to support me?

Moral of the story: A problem shared isn't a burden – it's a relief. And nine times out of ten, it's met with kindness, not eye rolls. So pick up the phone. You don't have to carry it alone. Even make some jokes in the process if it helps convey how you're feeling without the heavy talk – use humour to carry you and your feelings.

LOW MOODS

At night, many of us find ourselves scrolling on social media, and then wonder why we suddenly feel not good enough. It's no mystery – unrealistic snapshots of other people's lives have a sneaky way of burrowing into our minds, quietly whispering that we're falling short.

And while people love to say, *'Just change your mindset,'* anyone who's been in a low mood knows it's not that simple. Sometimes, the slump comes from real stuff – a set of circumstances, an email, or a text that hits like a massive letdown. And truly? Sometimes you just need to feel crap for a while. Sit in it. Feel it through. But at some point, there's got to be a moment where you decide to *feel it – then snap out of it.*

I've had plenty of days where I've tried everything to shake the heaviness, and nothing works in that moment. But it does pass. Eventually.

What's helped me, though? Tapping out. Physically switching

what I'm doing – changing what I'm engaging with. It's been a quiet little game changer.

The tricky part is that low moods love to keep us stuck. They'll offer some real 'helpful' suggestions like: isolate yourself, pour a drink, eat junk food, scroll until your thumb hurts. Pick your poison. It does this because the low mood feels safer than that of something new or uncertain. Remember, our brains don't like what they can't predict.

I'm a classic overthinker. If you're nodding along, I see you. It's exhausting, isn't it? Once those thoughts pick up speed, it's like being caught in a mental storm – spinning through fog you didn't ask for and feeling heavier by the minute. Even though deep down you know it will pass, in the moment it can feel like there's no way out. You're not alone in that space and, more importantly, you don't have to stay there.

The more we lean into those patterns, the stronger they become. It's like we train our brains to catastrophise for sport, and often there are bigger things at play that need addressing.

So what's the antidote? What works wonders for me? Tapping Out.

But here's the secret: you have to actually like what you're switching to. If juggling makes you roll your eyes, or the yo-yo reminds you of Year 5 trauma – scrap it. The whole point is to trigger those happy hormones, and that only happens if you're genuinely into it.

That's why your emotional toolkit needs to be full of your kind of joy. The stuff that lights you up.

Then take it a step further: schedule something fun. A solo playdate, or one with a friend. Anything that reminds your brain what lightness feels like.

Because when you're running low, your brain will try to send a signal. That quiet little voice is basically saying:

'Hey, Shan – we're running on empty. Time for a top-up.'

Listen to it.

When I'm in that sweet spot of motivation and flow, I always ask myself, 'Why can't I just flip that switch when I'm feeling down?' Like pressing a button that says, 'Let's go, feel good now!'

But here's the truth: when we're not feeling ourselves, flipping that switch feels nearly impossible. Instead, our minds rewind those old, painful mental movies – those moments we wish we could redo, the 'what ifs' that play on repeat.

Remember Rafiki from *The Lion King*, smacking Simba on the head and reminding him, 'It's in the past, it doesn't matter.' It's a gentle nudge to remind us that we don't have to keep fighting with yesterday's shadows. I'm a better version of myself than I was yesterday.

When your inner saboteur starts throwing punches – jab, jab, cross, hook – it's natural to want to retreat, to close off from the world and even from the things that normally light you up. That low mood might feel safe, but it's actually holding you back and draining your energy.

You don't have to fight alone or stay stuck. Even reaching out to one person who truly cares can be the lifeline that shifts everything. As impossible as it may feel, you have to reach.

So if you find yourself thinking, 'I'll call when I feel better,' know that courage isn't waiting for perfect feelings, it's reaching out anyway. It takes strength to break the cycle, but every small step forward is a victory.

You're not stuck; you're standing right at the edge, maybe hesitating. And what's waiting for you on the other side feels warmer, kinder, and so much more hopeful than those heavy feelings you've been carrying.

CHAPTER TWELVE

THE SECRECT WEAPON

Creativity is intelligence having fun.
- Albert Einstein -

Hey bosses and team leaders – want happier, more productive staff? Let them have fun.

Seriously. Play boosts creativity, motivation, and focus. A happy worker is a better worker. It doesn't need to be expensive or time-consuming – think hacky sacks, hula hoops, table tennis, or even a lunchtime office dance-off (participation optional, but encouraged).

And before you say, 'We don't have time' – yes, you do. We've muted our natural impulses at work, but play is still hardwired into us. It just needs a little nudge to come back to life.

Not everyone will be keen to bust a move in the break room, and that's okay. That's why variety matters. Offer a few options – table tennis, card games, puzzles. It's not about forcing fun. It's about giving people space to reset, connect, and recharge. Trust me, your team (and their productivity levels) will thank you.

Management teams, this is a must! Have you heard of the spacing effect? Basically, your brain needs a moment to process all the new stuff that just landed on its doorstep. That's where play breaks come in – they let your brain do its thing while you're having fun. And this isn't just fluff – science backs it. Giving your brain this little breather doesn't just help you remember stuff better; it has a ripple effect that perks up the rest of your body, too.

It's important to note that you never really know what someone's carrying when they walk through the door at work. Maybe they've just left behind marital stress, a health scare in the family, a teenager in full rebellion mode, or they're a sleep-deprived parent running on fumes. And let's not forget the peri- and menopausal women quietly wondering what on earth is going on with their bodies (spoiler: everything, all at once).

The point is, people show up. They turn up for work while juggling real, messy, complicated lives. So why not give them a chance to reset during the day? A bit of laughter, even five minutes of joy – these things can make a world of difference. You're not just boosting productivity; you're reminding your team they're human first.

Creativity and innovation thrive when people feel safe, energised, and seen. When people laugh together, they collaborate better. Happy brains think better.

MAGIC FLOW

When you're in the flow, it's pure magic – an optimal experience where everything just clicks. Playful moments are a perfect example of hitting that zone. Take my friend Denise, for instance. She's fifty-eight now and has loved dancing since forever. But back when she was twenty, she hit a tough fork in the road: either chase the dream of becoming a pro dancer or walk away. There was no middle ground. So, she stopped dancing. She told me, 'I quit because people told me I wouldn't make it. But that didn't mean I stopped loving it.' Fast forward thirty years, and Denise said, 'Every time I dance now, I feel electric – like I haven't felt in decades. I'm nicer to my body now than when I was younger.' And that's exactly what she does today: dances at her own pace, savouring those moments where she feels truly alive.

We've got to unshackle ourselves from the belief that certain parts of our lives are behind us forever. That what once was has no place in the present. That kind of thinking doesn't serve us, not one bit. You're the only one who knows if there's unfinished business tugging at you – those quiet nudges that whisper, 'Hey, maybe there's still something here.'

When you let your inhibitions fall away, even just for a moment, you tap into a kind of freedom that's rare and real. It's where you get to meet yourself again – without the filters, the pressure, the self-doubt. Just you, as you are. And in the wise words of John Armstrong:

'Whatever cheerful and serene supports the mind, supports the body too.'

THANKFULLY, EVERYONE IS DIFFERENT

Fun looks different for everyone. It's not one-size-fits-all. Some of us recharge through quiet, creative solitude – painting, gardening, journaling. Others come alive through movement, connection, or a little adventure. For me, I don't just have one kind of play. Some days it's playing games with Summer and Ollie; other times it's chasing that adrenaline rush – like flying around on a quad bike. Then there are the slower-paced moments, like paddleboarding.

When I paddleboard, sometimes I bring a friend and we chat the entire time. Other days, I go alone, just tuning in to the sounds of the water and my surroundings. And on those solo days, something kind of magical happens – I often find myself joined by dolphins. They'll swim around me, glide under my board, and simply be with me, just for a moment. Every now and then, I'll take Summer or Ollie out with me, and we've had those dolphin encounters together, but most of the time, it's just me.

And I always come back from those moments feeling lighter, happier, and completely at ease. That's when I know I've found something that puts me in flow. And that feeling alone is proof: this is one of my outlets, one of the ways I reconnect with myself.

For me, the beach is my happy place. I feel rejuvenated, calm, and inspired – I love the salty air and sand beneath my feet. But one of my friends, Nadia, can't stand it. Sand, saltwater, seaweed – yuck, no thanks! If I invited her to chill at the beach, she'd say, 'No thanks, have fun, bye!' But mention salsa dancing? She'd show up faster than I could blink, and she'd already be on the floor warming up. That's the beauty of being different. Finding your own kind of play – an outlet that truly suits you – is key. When you discover something you enjoy, you're guaranteed to add real value to your life.

So, here's a list of ideas. See if anything makes you go, 'mmm, maybe.' And hey, if none of them are for you? That's not failure – it's progress. Because figuring out what you don't enjoy is a solid step closer to discovering what you do. Think of it as trial and error.

> *The shoe that fits one person pinches another; there is no recipe for living that suits all cases.* **Carl Jung**

- Singing (and/or karaoke)
- Dancing
- Games using your imagination (kids or grandkids are great at helping you do this)
- Creativity
- Board games
- Spontaneity
- Living on the edge with an activity
- Finger painting (yes, really!)
- Playing with your pet
- Horse riding
- Playing with animals
- DIY crafts (macramé, candle-making, tie-dye)
- Watercolour painting or sketching in a park
- Pottery class (Ghost moment optional)

- Building Lego sets (adults-only themes exist!)
- Cooking for fun
- Trampoline park visit (bounce the stress away)
- Hula hooping in the backyard
- Roller skating or skateboarding
- Adult gymnastics or aerial silks class
- Paddleboarding or kayaking
- Rock climbing (indoor or outdoor)
- Car laps at a raceway
- Bike riding – leisurely or more adventurous if you want the rush
- Game nights (think Cards Against Humanity, Codenames, Uno with wild rules)
- Murder mystery dinner parties
- Trivia nights at a pub or DIY at home
- Escape rooms
- Improv class or comedy workshops
- Dungeons & Dragons or other roleplay games
- Giant bubble blowing (more fun than you'd expect)
- Stargazing with a telescope and snacks
- Building a blanket fort & reading inside it
- 'Yes Day' with a friend (say yes to all mini adventures)
- Trying on wild outfits at an op shop for fun
- Singing loudly in the car with the windows down (you'll look nuts, but it's so much fun)
- Tree climbing

- Barefoot walk on grass or sand
- Ziplining or quad biking
- Nature trail treasure hunt
- Gardening with music
- Calligraphy
- Flying a kite
- Mini golf or bowling in fancy dress
- Jumping in puddles or dancing in the rain
- Building a sandcastle like you mean it
- Finding joy in movement
- Watching cartoons on a Saturday morning with cereal (wrapped in a blanket)

FAKE FUN

Just a little heads-up: when you're exploring what is good outlet for you, it's easy to stumble into things that feel like they are doing the job … but actually aren't. Scrolling endlessly on your phone? Not a fun outlet. Deep diving into political debates? Important, sure – but not what we are looking for. Binge-watching your favourite show? Fun, but more of a wind-down than a spark-up.

Even activities like chores, caregiving, or a long soak in the bath – while lovely and often necessary – don't quite count. Traditional seated meditation and things with a set outcome (like creating art to sell) are beautiful practices, but they usually land in a different category. They're purposeful, yes – but not the kind of purposeless joy we're talking about here.

Real fun has no goal other than to feel good while you're doing it. It's about being in the moment, not producing something at the end. You might still get creative, sweaty, or inspired – but it's the joy, not the outcome, that matters.

And most importantly? Your version of play should be just for you – outside your job, your responsibilities, or your productivity. Just a little slice of light-hearted freedom.

WE ALL HAVE AN INNER REBEL

Being a rebel can be thrilling – but not the kind that hurts others. Be a rebel for yourself. For your freedom. When you find a kind of play that really suits you, magical things happen in your brain. The overthinking committee – self-criticism, anxiety, and perfectionism – finally takes a seat and quiets down for a bit. It's like hitting the mute button on that inner voice that says, 'You should be doing something productive!'

If you're someone who struggles to let things go, play can be your secret weapon. Why? Because it has no objective except joy. No gold stars. No performance reviews. Just permission to muck about, be a bit ridiculous, and actually enjoy yourself. Give your ego a nap and let your real self stretch its legs - you might just discover that nutty, glorious you is kind of awesome.

I failed to mention earlier that when we all agreed to go quad-bike riding, we decided to dress up as Mexican gangsters - for no reason whatsoever. Just for shits and giggles, really. One mention of the theme and we were off buying bandanas, fake tattoos, and flannelette shirts. The people at the quad-bike place asked, 'Oh, is this a hen party? A birthday party? Some event that requires this absurdity?' Nope - nothing. No reason at all. We just thought it would be funny. And holy heck, it was.

You don't need a reason - just a willingness to dial up the fun.

YOUR TONIC

You need a pause – a moment to breathe, stretch, and feel alive. Rick Rubin calls it the child inside, waiting to play and experience joy for joy's sake.

Kids don't overthink it. They laugh loudly, run for no reason, and follow their impulses. We adults? We bury that joy under to-do lists and expectations. But the closer we get to that childlike freedom, the lighter, freer, and more ourselves we feel.

Play is your secret weapon. It slashes stress, sparks creativity, sharpens your mind, and keeps your energy vibrant. It builds connection, ignites laughter, and turns awkward moments into magic. As Bashar says, 'You can only experience things that match the energy state you generate.' So play, laugh, create – and let yourself feel alive again.

CHAPTER THIRTEEN

YOUR SUPERPOWER

三つ子の魂百まで(みつご の たましい ひゃくまで)

A child's nature stays the same for life. **Japanese Proverb**.

The above Japanese proverb is one of my absolute favourites. It's a gentle reminder that the character and quirks we have at age three often stay with us throughout our lives. We don't grow out of ourselves – we just learn to block or filter those natural impulses that once drew us to play, silliness, and joy.

DIFFERENT STROKES

Not everyone finds the same things funny, and that's completely okay. The key is to find your kind of funny, and trust me, your people will meet you there.

For example, Dan listens to a podcast that he finds absolutely hilarious – me, not so much. The topics are great and super engaging for their target audience, but I don't happen to find locker-room banter among predominantly male sports players all that entertaining. Dan, however, will laugh so hard he nearly has to pull the car over because it becomes a public safety issue.

But that's the point. His mates love that kind of banter. Me? I'll be doubled over laughing when he trips over his own feet in the hallway. Different strokes, same belly laugh.

PHONES AREN'T PLAYMATES

So, if you've identified something that you want to get stuck into, first thing is first – pop your phone to the side. Be present with what you're doing – not one arm in and one arm out, thinking that you're missing out on something. I say this with love: phones aren't play. Not scrolling, not games, not the endless rabbit hole of 'just one more reel.' Sorry to be the bearer of bad news, but it's true. As mentioned previously, studies show that even just having your phone nearby can raise anxiety levels. It's like your brain's on edge, waiting for a ding.

But look, phones aren't evil. They're a tool. If they help you jot down notes, look something up, or find a new trail to explore on your bike – great! Even a bit of banter in the group chat or texting a friend to schedule some actual fun? Brilliant. But play – real, soul-stretching, joy-giving play, asks for more presence than that screen can offer.

GRATITUDE + A FUN OUTLET = YOUR SECRECT WEAPON

Life's messy. Toast burns, coffee spills, socks vanish into the mysterious sock vortex (along with all your hair ties). Gratitude is like slipping into your comfiest slippers – it makes the chaos a little easier to bear. Notice the small wins – like most of your coffee stayed in the cup – and suddenly the big annoyances shrink. Bonus: gratitude boosts happiness, lowers stress, and makes you grumble at the toaster less.

Layer in fun, and life lights up. Dance in your kitchen, chase your dog, build a puzzle, start a prank war – it all sparks creativity, loosens tension, builds connection, and makes you feel alive.

Here's the kicker: your real power is choice. Pick your fun – deep passions, mini adventures, silly bursts of joy. These are the tools that yank you out of the daily grind and remind you why you're here: to feel, to experience, to discover what lights up your soul.

You'll know you've hit the sweet spot when your body feels lighter, your mind clearer, and somewhere deep down you whisper, 'Yes.

More of this, please.'

BURNT TOAST THEORY

Have you ever heard of the Burnt Toast Theory? Long story short: I was coming up to the traffic lights, ready to turn right, and in front of me was an old man on his bike. I was in a rush to get home and chatting to my sister on the phone at the same time. Well, this old man took so long to pedal his bike around the corner, he even stopped to take in the view before continuing on – his dawdling meant I missed my turn and the lights turned red. And then? He turned the other way, which meant he didn't even need to use that lane in the first place.

'FAR OUT! WHAT IS THIS GUY DOING?' I yelled into my sister's ear.

Without missing a beat, she blurted back: 'BURNT TOAST!'

I said, 'What the hell are you talking about? What does that have to do with the slow old man who was in the wrong turning lane?'

She explained that she'd seen it on TikTok and felt I needed to hear it.

The Burnt Toast Theory is the idea that when something inconvenient or annoying happens, like burning your toast, missing a green light, or getting stuck behind someone moving at a glacial pace, it might actually be life, the universe, or something bigger protecting you from something you'll never even know about. Spiritually, it's the belief that delays, detours, and disruptions aren't just random – they're redirections. That missed turn? Maybe it saved you from being in the wrong place at the wrong time. That burnt toast? Maybe it slowed you down just enough to avoid something you weren't meant to cross paths with. It's about trusting that sometimes the 'no' or the 'not yet' is actually a quiet 'I've got you' from the universe. So instead of spiralling when things go sideways, we can pause, take a breath, and say, 'Maybe this is just my burnt toast moment.'

DEEP FORMS

1. **Improvisational Theatre or Role-Playing**
   Fully stepping into a character or spontaneous scenario requires emotional openness, quick thinking, and collaboration.

2. **Creative Arts**
   Painting, sculpting, writing, music composition, or dance that flows from an internal impulse rather than external pressure.

3. **Long-form Board Games or Strategy Games**
   Games that require patience, planning, and social interaction over extended periods.

4. **Outdoor Exploration & Adventure**
   Activities like hiking, climbing, kayaking, or mountain biking challenge your body and mind while immersing you in nature.

5. **Deep Conversations & Storytelling**
   Engaging in meaningful dialogue or sharing stories that build empathy and connection.

6. **Mindful Movement Practices**
   Tai Chi, or martial arts practised with full awareness and intention.

7. **Building or Crafting Projects**
   Woodworking, DIY projects, or even coding, activities that require sustained focus and problem-solving.

8. **Team Sports or Dance**
   Sports or dance that require synchrony, trust, and cooperation with others over time.

These forms of play not only refresh you but often help develop skills, relationships, and a deeper understanding of yourself and others. What kind of deep play interests you most?

QUICK FORMS

1. Dancing to a favourite song – crank up the music and move however you feel, even if it's just for a minute or two.

2. Silly faces or jokes with friends or family – quick laughter is a powerful reset.

3. Playing catch or tossing a ball around – even a few throws can get you moving and connecting.

4. Jumping on a trampoline or doing a few jumping jacks – instant energy boost.

5. Quick improv games – word association or 'what if' scenarios that spark creativity.

6. Short bursts of playful texting or banter – exchanging funny memes, GIFs, or jokes with friends.

7. Mini scavenger hunts or playful challenges – find something red in the room, or do five quick stretches.

8. Playing with a pet – a few minutes of chasing a ball or cuddling.

9. Mindless doodling or colouring – a quick creative release.

10. Trying a funny new dance trend – just because.

These quick fun forms can fit between meetings, during breaks, or anytime you need a little lift. They're simple but can make a big difference in how you feel. You'll know when it hits that sweet spot – you'll be motivated to chase that feeling.

THROW SOME FUN BAIT

Start with curiosity. Try something new. Invite someone into the experience – throw some 'play bait' out to a mate, your spouse, your kids, your parents. 'Want to come for a walk?' 'Let's sign up for that pottery class.' Being persistent and present is key.

Have you ever played the game Snog, Marry, Kill? It's dark humour, and I play it with Dan regularly. It's where you're given three people – usually celebrities or mutual friends – and you must decide who you'd snog, who you'd marry, and who you'd, well ... kill.

We once played it using schoolteachers we know – oh gosh, comedy gold when you ask why someone chose a particular teacher. It forces you straight into fantasy land, and honestly, it's just so funny. Suddenly, I'm picturing who is making eggs in the kitchen when I get up, saying, 'Morning, love!'

Your fun outlets can be solo or shared. Large groups often break into smaller ones, and that's okay – it's about connection, not crowd size. Watch out for the fun police, though – you know the type. The ones who roll their eyes or scoff when you're enjoying yourself. Simply ignore them and keep going.

WHAT ARE WE SEEKING?

We're seeking joy. Laughter. The kind of presence that wipes away your to-do list. Excitement, awe, aliveness. Energy. That rare, beautiful thing: being fully yourself.

YOUR FUN WILL LOOK DIFFERENT

To some, mountain biking is madness. To others, a pottery wheel is just spinning mud. It doesn't matter. What lights you up is what matters. And often, it builds community along the way. Volunteering, for example, is proven to boost memory, improve mood, and deepen our sense of connection – not because it's 'productive,' but because it's meaningful.

MOVE YOUR BODY - IT'S BUILT FOR IT

You don't need to go 'hardcore' or buy into the 'no pain, no gain' culture. Unless you're training for the Olympics, why are we glorifying suffering? Moving your body should feel good. It's not about punishment – it's about expression.

There is nothing more humbling – or a faster way to bring my ass thudding back down to earth – than when my kids catch me dancing in the kitchen. At first, I don't hear them because the music's blasting in my ears, and, last I saw, they were deep into their favourite TV show. Then comes the tap on the shoulder.

'MUM ... what are you doing?'

As corny as it sounds, I just say, 'Having a good old dance to Aretha Franklin.' Cue the eye roll – and off they go. But secretly, I know it's doing something. It's giving them quiet permission to follow what feels natural and lights them up.

I've even caught Summer dancing in her room before. I poked my head in, saw she was having a great time, and naturally joined in – I threw my hands in the air and off I went. She clocked me instantly and frog-marched me straight out of her room and into the hallway – wow, what a thrilling moment for me. If you were a fly on the wall, you'd have wet yourself laughing at my expense.

But here's the thing: the more I drop my guard and let that joy out, the more she knows it's okay to do the same – even if I do get kicked out every now and then.

Dancing is just gold – either do it alone or with others. Bodies moving in sync, or bouncing off each other's energy – that's the good stuff. Since the beginning of time, people have danced to awaken the self, mark rituals, honour passion, and reconnect to something bigger than themselves. You lose yourself, and at the same time, you find a deeper version of you.

Music supports all of this. Slow music can lower your blood pressure. Upbeat dance tracks? They raise your heart rate and help lower stress hormones like cortisol. Even better, when we listen to music together, our brains actually sync up in the areas that process emotion, language, and delight. That's a real connection – right there in the beat.

Music is identity, too. You can often tell a lot about someone by the music they love (and the stickers on their car, too). If someone looks a certain way or falls into a particular age group, you might take a guess at their favourite genre. But if a ninety-year-old woman tells you she's into thrash metal? Tell me you wouldn't instantly want to hear her life story.

WHY IT FEELS SO GOOD

When you move, when you laugh, when you play – you shift your whole vibration. Literally. Your body starts to hum at a higher frequency. And when you're up there, joy has an easier time finding you.

One of my best pals, Natty, was diagnosed with breast cancer. And like so many of life's hardest moments, it cracked something open in her - not just fear, but clarity. Bit by bit, she began finding her way back to parts of herself she may not have noticed for years.

Following her curiosity led her to her version of play: pottery. Clay under her nails, mind clear, spirit lifted - it grounded her. But it wasn't just the art. It was the way she allowed herself to embrace every form of healing available to her. She worked with her oncologist, breast surgeon, naturopath, and acupuncturist. She allowed herself to choose joy, to take weekends away with her girl gang, to laugh loudly, to rest deeply, and to tend to every layer of who she is.

Through it all, she grew gentler and more attuned to herself - learning to give her needs space, attention, and importance in a way she never had before.

Her courage, her softness, and her willingness to follow what lights her up have inspired me deeply. And I hope they inspire you too - a reminder that sometimes the hardest chapters guide us back to our truest selves, and that play, in all its forms, isn't frivolous - it's fuel.

THIS IS A LONG-TERM RELATIONSHIP

Fun and movement aren't just for the moment – they're about mental health, resilience, and sticking around in one piece. Life feels lighter when you keep moving, even a little.

Chronic pain can make activity feel impossible, like it's for someone else. But gentle movement is powerful. Work *with* your body, not against it. Curious about dancing, swimming, or gardening? Give it a go. Make a list, bring it to your healthcare provider, and if they aren't on board, find someone who gets it. You deserve care that supports your whole self.

Aches and creaks come for all of us eventually, but regular movement can soften the blow. It doesn't need to be a workout – a walk with a friend, a stretch class, or dancing while cooking counts. Movement is medicine, and doing it with someone you trust adds joy, connection, and maybe even world-problem-solving along the way.

The trick? Consistency, curiosity, and kindness toward your body – even on the hard days. Especially on the hard days.

If any part of this chapter sparked curiosity, take that seriously. That feeling is trying to tell you something. Follow it. Joy and playful activities aren't frivolous; they are foundational. They might just be the thing that helps you remember who you are, underneath the deadlines, the roles, the expectations.

When we think about fun and how we engage in it, Jonathan Haidt's work offers an interesting perspective. In his book, Jonathan talks about how women tend to connect through talking (yes, those three-hour debriefs over coffee are biologically backed) and often have a more detailed mental map of social space, like emotional cartographers. Meanwhile, boys are generally more interested in physical objects, things they can build, fix, throw, or launch off a makeshift ramp. Neither is better. It's not a competition. It just shows we're wired differently, and that's what makes life interesting.

One group's idea of a good time might be a deep-and-meaningful conversation on the couch; the other might call it bonding while quietly reviewing 'controversial umpiring decisions' from ten years ago with a mate. Both are valid forms of play. Just don't make them swap seats.

Fun that gets your heart pumping – even just a little – can actually help flush out cortisol, that stress hormone that shows up uninvited like a seagull at a beach picnic. You know the feeling: you're halfway through a kitchen dance-off or wildly chasing a runaway shopping trolley in the car park, and suddenly, you're not as tightly wound. That's your body letting go. Movement, especially the kind you enjoy, does wonders – not just for your brain, but for your whole system. We're talking real, science-backed benefits like lowered risk of cardiovascular disease, anxiety, depression, cancer, and autoimmune conditions.

And hey, if you're someone who loves sprinting up hills for fun, you do you. But for the rest of us, just find something that feels good and makes you smile. Walk your dog with music in your ears. Kick a ball. Jump in the ocean. It's not about intensity; it's about consistency and enjoyment. The more fun you have moving, the more likely you are to keep doing it. And once you're in that zone, it's wild how many other good things start lining up too.

Going forward, it really is a commitment to investing in yourself; it does take self-awareness and allowing yourself to pause when things come up that don't sit well with you. The best remedy is to ask yourself questions: Is this helping or hindering me? Am I being authentically me? Does this relationship serve and support me to be the best version of myself?

If curiosity is baiting you toward finding a form of play that allows you to have a release, being aware of certain types of emotions that stand in your way is helpful. Put some space between you and the thought, because you aren't your emotions, and they, in turn, aren't you. Suppose the emotion you are feeling is a concern because you have knee problems and feel it could stand in your way. In that case, that's where, instead of pulling away altogether, you can do your research and find out how modifications can be made to suit your body in its present state. So you see, the concern offered you some information you may like to consider, but it didn't give you the whole story.

CHAPTER FOURTEEN
FREE YOURSELF FROM THE CHAINS THAT BIND ~ Chaka Khan

What you do speaks louder than what you say
~ **Jack Canfield & Mark Victor Hansen, Chicken Soup for the Soul** ~

The generation below you is always watching – especially when you think they're not.

Trust me, they're clocking it all: how you handle stress, joy, failure … even a dodgy parallel park.

And it's easy to assume the attention only flows one way – from younger eyes watching us. But it doesn't. Most of us are still quietly tuned into the generation above us, too. I know I am … front row, popcorn in hand, watching the Boomer Show unfold.

My friend Alana and I love comparing the 'us versus them' quirks, and no doubt the generation coming up will do the same with us. Humour helps here – it lets some air out of the tyres without stressing over what we can't control.

I take note of what's working for them and where they might be stuck in the 'but this is how we've always done it' mindset. Sometimes that still works. And sometimes it's like watching someone try to use a flip phone to navigate Google Maps.

Children, in particular, live what they learn. They soak up the emotional tone of a household faster than a sponge in a bathtub. We can say all the right things, but if our actions don't line up?

They notice. And they store that information for later, sometimes decades later. It would be naïve of us to think we're done learning just because we've hit a certain age or milestone. Growth isn't reserved for the young. We're all in this weird, beautiful cycle of learning and unlearning, right up until the day the curtain falls, and we take our final bow.

So yes, we watch our children. We worry, we guide, and we may shake our heads at their questionable life choices and TikTok dances. But rest assured, they're watching us too. They're watching to see what we do with our one wild and precious life. They're paying attention to how we treat people, how we speak about ourselves, how we handle change. They're listening when we talk about our dreams – or when we say we're 'too old' to chase them.

Also, what messages are we passing down to the younger generation? It's unlikely they'll look back and admire us for our relentless work ethic or burnout culture. That's not a legacy to be proud of – it's a reminder that something needs to change if we truly want longer, healthier lives with more quality in them. The good news is, we have the chance to model something better – balance, rest, and a way of living that makes space for joy.

I'm a big believer that life gives us what we need to know right when we need to know it. Sometimes that wisdom comes in the form of a child's question that stops us in our tracks. Sometimes it's a passing comment from an older relative that hits harder than expected. The point is: everyone's watching, and everyone's teaching – even when they don't mean to be. So the question becomes, what are we modelling – and what are we still open to learning?

ACTION FIRST, FEELING LATER

Have fun first. Laugh first. Then the good feelings follow. It's not the other way around.

We so often fall into the trap of thinking, 'I'll enrol in that dance class when I feel better … when I have more time … when everything settles down.' But here's the truth: you won't feel better first. You do the thing, and the feeling shows up after.

We've got to unshackle ourselves from this old belief that joy is a reward you get only after surviving the chaos or ticking off every task. Nope! Joy – play – laughter – being content is the fuel that gets you moving, thinking clearly, and feeling like your best self.

Start now. Notice the little things that spark your curiosity or make you smile. (Pro tip: jot them down when they come, because when you finally have 'free time,' your brain might just blank out and say, 'Netflix, anyone?').

And, when you let yourself prioritise your happiness, it becomes contagious. Suddenly, you're the person who brings a little lightness wherever you go. No preaching needed. Just showing up as someone who chooses joy first.

So when you ask, what are my priorities? The answer is simple:

Your happiness. Start there.

Your body's been ready to party this whole time. It knows what feels good, what makes you laugh-snort, what brings that spark back. Meanwhile, your brain's still in a meeting about whether play is 'productive enough.' Bless it. Sometimes, your head just needs a gentle shove from your heart (or a dance break) to remember: joy isn't a luxury – it's a full-body yes.

EUDAIMONIA ISN'T JUST A BUZZ WORD

An ancient Greek word – Eudaimonia translates roughly to 'human flourishing,' a contented state of being happy, healthy, and prosperous. Aristotle called it the highest human good, the ultimate goal of a life well lived. It's not just a fancy word; it's a reminder of what life can be when you align yourself with your deepest self.

It's not honourable to dismiss yourself. Albert Einstein once said, 'A ship is always safe at the shore, but that's not what it's built for.' Think about that. You were built for experiences. To venture out, to explore, to indulge in all the messy, wonderful chaos of living. This is your God-given right, your birthright.

Life isn't something that just happens to you. It's something you create, moment by moment. Desire ... ask ... believe ... receive. (Thanks, Stella Terrill-Mann, for putting it so succinctly.)

Think of Charles Dickens. Even though we 'read' his words with our minds, the real magic – the seed of artistic delight – is that tingling feeling between your shoulder blades, the shivers, the goosebumps that run down your arms and neck, maybe even the crown of your head. Something washes over you, and suddenly you're part of something bigger. That's the magic of emotional contagion, the power of shared consciousness and community.

This is exactly what we're aiming for. It's all part of the grand human experience – connection, joy, discovery.

You need to believe you are allowed to gift yourself this time. You need to claim a sense of entitlement – not in a selfish way, but in a bold, internal-gumption kind of way that says, 'This is my right. I deserve to take care of myself. I get to explore what fits me best.' You're allowed to have a voice, a vision, and yes – a little bit of admirable arrogance in saying, 'I matter.'

WISDOM GROWS

As we get older, it's clear that wisdom grows, and so does our willingness to give fewer damns about what others think. Honestly, most people are too busy living their own lives to be bothered about yours. And that's freeing! As an adult, you finally get the perspective to truly appreciate what brings you joy. You get the chance to make something of yourself and make something with yourself.

Remember, you'll be at your 'max capacity' – your fullest self – on the day you die.

SO, WHAT'S YOUR NEXT MOVE?

Maybe it's dusting off that old guitar you haven't touched since college. Or joining a local dance class where you can laugh more than worry about stepping on toes. Perhaps it's hiking a new trail, feeling the earth beneath your feet, and watching the sunset paint the sky like a masterpiece just for you.

Or maybe it's something delightfully simple, like blowing bubbles in the backyard, chasing after your dog, or hosting a game night with friends that turns into a laughter marathon. It doesn't matter if it's big or small, messy or graceful. What matters is that you have more fun.

GAMING (Don't Shoot the Messenger)

Neuroscientist Stephen Porges puts it simply: we're meant to play and connect with people – not just with phones or consoles. As humans, we're wired for face-to-face interaction. It's the eye contact, the inside jokes, the spontaneous belly laughs that build trust and make us feel safe with each other.

But here's the twist – the very tech we've welcomed in for convenience and entertainment often gets in the way. Instead of bringing us closer, our screens can quietly block the real-life moments we need most.

Gaming and social media may offer a version of connection, but it's a limited one – often performative, curated, and emotionally diluted. It lacks the warmth of touch, the nuance of facial expression, the spark of unfiltered, in-the-moment joy. Our minds and bodies know this instinctively. That's why so many of us feel the disconnection, the loneliness, the mental exhaustion – even when we're 'connected' online. Because we're missing something essential: presence. Bonding. Real-time interaction with real people, in the flesh.

This is not about demonising tech – it's about recognising the cost of using it as a replacement for the kind of play and connection our nervous systems crave. Our declining mental health isn't just a by-product of busy schedules – it's a biological signal that something vital is missing. And that something is human.

We're not machines. We glitch. We cry at insurance ads. We get overwhelmed, distracted, and sometimes we forget why we walked into a room ... or why we started something in the first place. Life throws in pain, insecurity, and a whole heap of weird feelings – that's the fine print of being human.

YOU HAVE TO TAKE THE FIRST STEP

Wouldn't it be nice if we could press a button and have our emotional mess tidied up? Sadly, there's no Marie Kondo for the soul. You've got to be the one to dig through the mental junk drawer and decide what actually sparks joy – and what's just emotional clutter taking up precious space.

I spent *years* trying to 'find my thing,' watching everyone else nail theirs – like they popped out of the womb knowing they were meant to practise law, throw pottery, or start kombucha empires. Meanwhile, I was over here trying on careers like last-minute Halloween costumes. I just wanted to be great at something, but of course, I missed the obvious: what I was already good at.

Turns out, my strengths weren't shiny LinkedIn skills or fancy titles. They were connection, humour, warmth – and telling stories that made people say, 'Oh my God, SAME.' That was my gold. I just couldn't see it while I was busy auditioning for roles I was never meant to play.

Here's the plot twist: being fully yourself – even the slightly chaotic, too-honest version – is more than enough. Especially if you can laugh while doing it.

And about those voices in your head whispering that you're not enough? They're not even yours. They're echoes from other people's fears, expectations, and outdated rules. Let them float by like bad elevator music; background noise, not the soundtrack.

Real self-awareness starts with one tiny question: *How does this feel for me?* That's it. That's the magic reset.

If you want a masterclass in emotional intelligence, watch a toddler. They feel everything – loudly – seek comfort and then move on like nothing happened. That's emotional freedom. No guilt, no overthinking. Just raw, glorious humanness.

Maybe we could all use a little more of that.

BOUNDARIES ARE BRIDGES NOT WALLS

Love doesn't mean always saying yes, and keeping the peace doesn't mean shrinking yourself to avoid the waves. Too often, we mistake kindness for silence – especially when something inside us senses that something's off. That's where confusion sneaks in. As author Adam Grant says, 'I need time for my confusion,' because confusion isn't just a jumble; it's a sign that new ground is being broken, a fresh puzzle waiting to be solved.

Those confusing moments usually pop up right when we're trying to figure out our boundaries. Boundaries aren't walls to keep people out; they're more like maps helping us explore new territory. But we often get it wrong and think they're selfish or harsh. So instead, we soften, we bend, we give more than we really have – even when it drains us.

I've been there – feeling drained, losing track of who I really am under all the expectations. But here's what I've learned: boundaries are actually bridges. They help us move through the messy confusion, reconnect with ourselves, and show up honestly – not just tolerating but really being present. Setting boundaries doesn't mean you're letting others down. It means you're showing up for your own truth.

For me, setting these boundaries has been a game-changer for my emotional well-being, especially as an empath who absorbs everyone's vibes like a sponge.

FINAL WORDS

Everyone has the chance to be young, but not everyone is awarded the gift of growing old.

'We learn in stillness so we remember when the storm comes.' This beautiful quote comes from Björn Natthiko Lindeblad, a former forest monk who offered deep compassion and insight into our often restless 'monkey minds.'

He reminds us that the tools we learn in quiet moments – when life feels calm – are the ones we'll need most when our storms arrive. And they will come. No one is exempt.

The trick is discovering which tools genuinely resonate with you, what can pull you out of heavy moods, break through stuck feelings, or fill that quiet emptiness inside. Often, we hold ourselves back from chasing what we truly want because, deep down, we believe we're not worthy of having it. I love telling stories – in case you hadn't already noticed.

And this is a little reminder that your stories matter, too. The joy you've experienced, the moments that shaped you, the things you're still figuring out – there's so much wisdom in the stories we don't share.

Follow what gently pulls at your curiosity. Notice what might be holding you back, and if you can, start loosening its grip. Make space for yourself. Truly – you're worth your own time.

It might sound strange that we even have to say that, but if you look at how many things we place ahead of our own happiness, it starts to make sense.

When those old thoughts creep in, 'I should have known better' –

try softening them into, 'Now I know better.' That small shift is a kind way of honouring how much you've grown.

Life can easily slip into routines, to-do lists, and autopilot. But when we take a step back and reconnect with what feels meaningful, everything else starts to shift. Research even tells us: the more meaning we find in life, the better our overall well-being becomes.

So take this as a quiet invitation to get to know yourself again. To tell your story in your own time and way.

Because what a privilege it is to meet yourself and maybe it's properly for the first time.

I read this at my Granny's funeral:

'Your footsteps may fade, but the path remembers. For having walked here once, you remain always.'

I don't want to sound morbid, but I've come to believe there's an unexpected beauty in death. It strips things back. It sharpens what really matters.

In the end, the people who love you won't talk about how busy you were, how many boxes you ticked, or how much you gave until there was nothing left.

They'll talk about your laugh.

Your spark.

The way your eyes lit up when you talked about something you loved.

Your quirks, your courage, your stories.

They'll remember the things that made you you.

That's what stays behind. Not the errands. Not the striving. Not the perfection.

But the joy.

The aliveness.

The moments you allowed yourself to just be.

We all want to matter in some way – to leave a mark. But in the end, it's not about achievement. It's about presence. It's the memories we leave in the spaces we once filled. The energy we imprint through laughter, kindness, curiosity, and the courage to be fully ourselves.

So maybe the question isn't just, what are we leaving behind?

But does it reflect who we truly are?

People will remember how you made them feel. The warmth of your laugh – or how brilliantly infectious it was. The quiet ways you showed up when it mattered. The small moments that somehow felt big.

So take more photos and videos.

Laugh until it hurts.

Tell the stories.

Say the thing.

And please – listen to the advice you give to others. We're often kinder, wiser, and more compassionate to everyone but ourselves. Start taking your own good advice.

Because you deserve to live in a way that your path remembers you well.

Every person stands between two worlds – the one they came from and the one they are creating for those who follow. By honouring yourself, you are honouring those who came before you and making it better for those who come after.

Confidence doesn't come from saying sweet things to yourself in the mirror.

It's built from a pile of undeniable proof – moments where you showed up, even when doubt was loud.

I truly believe the real test of self-love is whether we love ourselves enough not just to accept our flaws, but to fully embrace them.

And remember: your dreams are bigger than your fears.

Change is not something to fear – it's a chance to start fresh.

The best things in life aren't just given to us.

They're earned, fought for, and held close – the reward of showing up for yourself, day after day.

The world is changing – and it's not without its bumps. Lately, we've seen more behaviour that's all about 'me first'– people insisting they're always right, acting entitled or arrogant, and sometimes even crossing into bullying. It can feel noisy, competitive, and disconnected.

But instead of blaming anyone, it helps to see this as a sign that something's out of balance – especially between masculine and feminine energies, which have been out of sync for thousands of years. Neither masculine energy nor feminine energy is bad or fragile; the problem comes when one overshadows the other. When that happens, we lose the harmony that brings calm, empathy, and real respect.

What the world really needs isn't more ego – it needs balance. Like yin and yang, alpha and omega, strength and softness, these energies are both essential. Together, they create a complete circle – a more grounded, cooperative way of living.

And here's the hopeful part: that shift is already happening. More and more people are waking up, questioning old ways, and choosing connection over competition, presence over performance. This is how we start building a world where everyone feels heard, valued, and free to be their true, whole selves.

THE MARVELLOUS MYSTERY OF BECOMING

We never really know any of this for sure, but here's a hunch: the universe never stands still – it's always moving, shifting, changing. Like waves or clouds, it's never quite the same.

When you get that, you stop trying to control everything and let yourself be a little messy, a little unfinished.

Because we're always growing, always becoming – never done.

We shapeshift. We change. That's not failure – that's growth. And sometimes things need to break down to become stronger again.

And in this constant becoming, there's one universal desire that threads through us all: the longing to be understood. To be seen clearly without needing to explain or justify who we are. But for so many, even those closest to us – our family, our friends – struggle to understand us. That can hurt. It can isolate. But it also invites us to seek out our true selves. A tribe. A circle that feels like home. People who don't just laugh with us, but can laugh at themselves too. That's where the magic lives – in shared joy and unfiltered connection.

True beauty starts with being at ease in your own skin. That quiet inner voice – the one that loops endlessly in the background – speaks louder and more often than any words you say out loud. It's powerful, fertile ground. So treat it kindly. Nurture your mind as you would a child or a dear friend. And along the way? Remember, you don't need to step on others to rise. As Wayne Dyer wisely said, how people treat you is their karma; how you respond is yours. That's real power. That's true integrity.

Of course, it takes time and care to truly know who we are. The world is constantly shouting: be this, not that. Look like this, not that. Speak up, sit down. No wonder we doubt ourselves. But what if we loosened our grip on needing to look 'put together' all the time? Who are we performing for – and more importantly, who really cares?

We've inherited freedoms fought for by those who came before us. Let's honour that gift, not by chasing perfection, but by living fully. To laugh, to play, to fall apart and gather the pieces again. Because pain? It's part of the journey. You can't skip it or soar above it. You have to walk right through it. That's what makes the story rich. That's where strength is born.

And as Lauryn Hill said, 'Even my mother and father don't know me, heck, I don't even know me. I'm still getting to know me.'

Aren't we all?

Being human is a gift. A strange, beautiful, occasionally gut-wrenching gift. You don't have to be everything. You don't have to master every art form. Maybe you're not the one with the discipline to paint – but maybe you're the one who notices the tiny absurdities of the world and turns them into laughter. That's art too.

In the end, it's the same things that make life long that make life worth living – connection, curiosity, joy, a sense of purpose, and permitting yourself to do what lights you up.

Time is precious. And if we use it well, we've got more of it than we think.

Experience what feels good to you. That's not indulgent. That's being alive.

And you, my dear friend, deserve to be happy. The rest is yours to write. x

ACKNOWLEDGEMENTS

I am deeply humbled and genuinely grateful to the people in my corner who helped bring this book to life. You are my front-row people.

Firstly, and without hesitation – my Dannyboy. Your love and unwavering support in all that I do mean more to me than you'll ever know. I know you've carried my stresses and worries without me even asking. Thank you for believing in me and for making me laugh when I needed it most. You're my rock, and I love you.

To my kids, Summer and Ollie - without even realising it, you are my greatest teachers. I love you more than life itself, and I'm so proud of you.

To my family - Mum, Dad, and Steph - thank you for your patience in knowing that I had a path I needed to follow. It wasn't an easy one, but thank you for loving and backing me no matter what. I'm so blessed to have you.

To my UK family and friends - thank you for your love and support from across the waters.

To my business partner, friend, and favourite sicko, Tamara - I love what we create together.

To my soul sisters - the ones who fiercely support everything I do, squeal the loudest, and always tell me to keep chasing my dreams. You've stood by me through everything, and we all know it's because we signed that contract that means we're bound for life. Alana, Sammy, Kay, Nadia, Natalie, Adriana, Tanya, Laura, Cassie, Deanna, Erin, Tracy, Amber, Justine, Megan, Bec, Gemma, Sanja, my girl-hangs crew, my Redstar faves, my cheer and dance community - and so many more beautiful people I'm blessed to call friends.

To the team at 2QT Publishing - Catherine, it was as if you and your team were delivered straight to my door, perfectly packaged with the right ingredients: patience, kindness, and creativity. Thank you for helping shape this book and guiding it into the world so beautifully.

Thank you to everyone who has stood by my side - you know who you are, and you are magic. Every phone call, message, opening of doors, and unwavering support for me throughout my career and life have been etched into my heart.

Last but certainly not least - thank you to you, my dear reader. Without you, my book doesn't have legs. I'm deeply grateful that, for whatever reason, it found its way to you.

REFERENCES

A

Alzheimer's Association. 2023 Alzheimer's Disease Facts and Figures. Alzheimer's & Dementia, 19(4), 1598–1695, 2023. Available at https://www.alz.org/media/Documents/alzheimers-facts-and-figures-2023-r.pdf.

Aristotle. *Nicomachean Ethics*. Translated by Terence Irwin, 2nd edition, Hackett Publishing Company, 2009.

Attia, Dr Peter. *Outlive: The Science and Art of Longevity*. Vermilion, 2023.

B

Barrett, Lisa Feldman. *How Emotions Are Made: The Secret Life of the Brain*. Houghton Mifflin Harcourt, 2017.

Bartlett, Steven. *The Diary of a CEO: 'The Miracle Doctor: Everyone Should Start Fasting Right Now!'* Episode 256, 15 June 2023. Available at Spotify.

Benartzi, Shlomo. *The Brain and Stress: The Adaptive Brain*. Pergamon Press, 1983.

Berk, L. S., et al. *Neuroendocrine and stress hormone changes during mirthful laughter*. American Journal of the Medical Sciences, 298(6), 390–396, 1989.

Blanchflower, David G., and Andrew J. Oswald. *Is Well-Being U-Shaped over the Life Cycle?* Social Science & Medicine, 66(8), 1733–1749, 2008.

Blood, A. J., & Zatorre, R. J. Intensely pleasurable responses to music correlate with activity in brain regions implicated in reward and emotion. Proceedings of the National Academy of Sciences, 98(20), 11818–11823, 2001.

Brach, Tara. *Radical Acceptance: Embracing Your Life With the Heart of a Buddha.* Bantam, 2003.

Brown, Brené. *Atlas of the Heart: Mapping Meaningful Connection and the Language of Human Experience.* Random House, 2021.

Brown, Stuart. *Play: How It Shapes the Brain, Opens the Imagination, and Invigorates the Soul.* Avery, 2009.

Buettner, Dan. *Live to 100: Secrets of the Blue Zones.* Netflix, 2023. Available at netflix.com/au/title/81214929.

C

Cacioppo, John T., and Louise Cacioppo. *Loneliness: Human Nature and the Need for Social Connection.* W. W. Norton & Company, 2018.

Canfield, Jack, and Mark Victor Hansen. *Chicken Soup for the Soul: 20th Anniversary Edition.* HCI Books, 2013.

Coelho, Paulo. *The Alchemist.* Harper Collins, 1993.

D

Dattani, Saloni. *What is the lifetime risk of depression? Our World in Data, 18 May 2022.* Available at https://ourworldindata.org/depression-lifetime-risk.

Dispenza, Dr. Joe. *Rewired.* Gaia, 2019. Available at gaia.com/series/rewired

Dispenza, Dr Joe. *Becoming Supernatural: How Common People Are Doing the Uncommon.* Hay House, 2017

F

Filipino Humor and Death: Coping with Loss Through Laughter.

Taas Noo Pilipino, 2024. Available at https://taasnoopilipino.com/filipino-humor-and-death-coping-with-loss-through-laughter/.

Franklin, Shanelle, and Tamara Linke. *The Beautiful Nightmare: Interview with Georgie Carroll*. Episode released [2023]. Available at https://thebeautifulnightmare.com/podcast.

G

Garcia, Hector & Miralles, Francesc. Ikigai: *The Japanese Secret to a Long and Happy Life*. Penguin Life, 2017.

Ghanaian Funeral Traditions: How the Dead Are Celebrated. Tourispot Ghana, July 8, 2025. Available at https://tourispotghana.com/2025/07/08/how-ghana-celebrates-the-dead-funeral-traditions-explained/.

Grazer, Brian, and Charles Fishman. *A Curious Mind: The Secret to a Bigger Life*. Simon & Schuster, 2015.

H

Haidt, Jonathan. *The Anxious Generation: How the Great Rewiring of Childhood Is Causing an Epidemic of Mental Illness*. Penguin Press, 2024. ISBN 978-0-593-65503-0.

Harari, Yuval Noah. Sapiens: *A Brief History of Humankind*. Harper, 2015.

I

Inside Out 2. Directed by Kelsey Mann, produced by Pixar Animation Studios and Walt Disney Pictures, 2024.

K

Kang, Min Jeong, et al. *The wick in the candle of learning: Epistemic curiosity activates reward circuitry and enhances memory*. Psychological Science, 20(8), 963–973, 2009.

Kasser, Tim. *The High Price of Materialism*. MIT Press, 2002.

Keltner, Dacher. *Awe: The New Science of Everyday Wonder and How It Can Transform Your Life.* Penguin Press, 2023.

Kessler, David. *Finding Meaning: The Sixth Stage of Grief.* Scribner, 2002.

Khan, Chaka. *Free Yourself.* Warner Bros. Records, 1985.

L

Lindeblad, Björn Natthiko. *I May Be Wrong: And Other Wisdoms from Life as a Forest Monk.* Bloomsbury Publishing, 2022. ISBN 978-1526644848.

M

Mary Poppins. Directed by Robert Stevenson, performances by Julie Andrews and Dick Van Dyke, Walt Disney Productions, 1964.

Maté, G., & Maté, D. (2022). *The Myth of Normal: Trauma, Illness, and Healing in a Toxic Culture.* Vermilion.

Maté, Gabor. *When the Body Says No: The Cost of Hidden Stress.* Scribe Publications, 2019.

N

Neufeld, Gordon. *Hold On to Your Kids: Why Parents Need to Matter More Than Peers.* Ballantine Books, 2005.

Nørretranders, Tor. Hvælv – *Videnskabens Verdensbilleder: Jordens Gudinde* – Teorien om Gaia. Directed by Orla Harregaard, 1986. Available at IMDb.

P

Park, Bum-Jin, et al. The physiological effects of Shinrin-yoku (taking in the forest atmosphere or forest bathing): evidence from field experiments in 24 forests across Japan. Environmental Health and Preventive Medicine, 15(1), 18–26, 2010.

Parker, Dorothy. *The Portable Dorothy Parker.* Edited by Marion Meade, Penguin Books, 1960.

Purves, Dale, et al. *Neuroscience*, 6th Edition. Oxford University Press, 2018.

R

Reuters. Pope Francis meets world comedians, including Whoopi Goldberg. Reuters, June 8, 2024. Available at https://www.reuters.com/world/europe/pope-francis-meet-world-comedians-including-whoopi-goldberg-2024-06-08/.

Robbins, Mel. *The Let Them Theory: A Life-Changing Tool That Millions of People Can't Stop Talking About.* Hay House, 2024.

Rubin, Rick. *The Creative Act: A Way of Being.* Penguin Press, 2023.

S

Salthouse, Timothy A. *When Does Age-Related Cognitive Decline Begin?* Neurobiology of Aging, 30(4), 507–514, 2009.

Sapolsky, Robert M. *Why Zebras Don't Get Ulcers: The Acclaimed Guide to Stress, Stress-Related Diseases, and Coping.* 3rd Edition, Holt Paperbacks, 2004.

Shear, Jonathan B., et al. T*he Physiological Sigh: A Mechanism for Rapid Recovery from Acute Stress.* Journal of Neurophysiology, 123(2), 2020, 714–723.

Smith, Dr Julie. *Why Has Nobody Told Me This Before?* Michael Joseph, 2022.

T

The Wizard of Oz. Directed by Victor Fleming, performances by Judy Garland, Ray Bolger, and Margaret Hamilton, Metro-Goldwyn-Mayer, 1939.

Tolle, Eckhart. *The Power of Now: A Guide to Spiritual Enlightenment.*

New World Library, 1997.

Toraja Funeral Rites: Traditions and Ancestral Symbols. Terra Cultura, 2024. Available at https://terra-cultura.com/en/toraja-funeral-rites-traditions-and-ancestral-symbols/.

Tsabary, Dr Shefali. *A Radical Awakening: Turn Pain into Power, Embrace Your Truth, Live Free.* HarperCollins, 2021.

V

Volkow, Nora D., et al. *Neurobiologic Advances from the Brain Disease Model of Addiction.* New England Journal of Medicine, 374: 363-371, 2016.

W

Weaver, Libby. *Rational Nutrition: Eating for Energy, Balance, and Vitality.* Allen & Unwin, 2018.

Watt Smith, Tiffany. *Schadenfreude: The Joy of Another's Misfortune.* Wellcome Collection, 2018. ISBN 9781781259108.

Ware, Bronnie. *The Top Five Regrets of the Dying: A Life Transformed by the Dearly Departing.* Hay House, 2011.

'Where focus goes, energy flows' (Robbins, 2025).

Winfrey, Oprah. *SuperSoul Conversations: Interview with Byron Katie.* Episode released [2019]. Available at oprahdaily.com/podcast.

World Health Organization. *Noncommunicable Diseases.* Available at who.int/health-topics/noncommunicable-diseases.

www.ingramcontent.com/pod-product-compliance
Lightning Source LLC
LaVergne TN
LVHW091935070526
838200LV00068B/1287